A GUIDE BOOK
TO HIGHWAY 66

A GUIDE BOOK
TO HIGHWAY 66

By

JACK D. RITTENHOUSE

A FACSIMILE OF THE 1946 FIRST EDITION

University of New Mexico Press
Albuquerque

Library of Congress Cataloging-in-Publication Data

Rittenhouse, Jack D. (Jack DeVere), 1912–
    A guide book to Highway 66/by Jack D. Rittenhouse.
        p.   cm.
    "A facsimile of the 1946 first edition." Originally published:
Los Angeles, Calif.: J. D. Rittenhouse, 1946.
    ISBN 0-8263-1148-2
    1. West (U.S.)—Description and travel—
1880–1950—Guide-books.
    2. United States Highway 66—Guide-books.
    3. Automobiles—Road guides—West (U.S.)
    I. Title.
    II. Title: Guide book to Highway Sixty-six.
F595.R59   1989
917.3'04927—dc 19   89-4807

txr

PREFACE TO FACSIMILE EDITION

This is an exact facsimile of the first guidebook of its kind for the full length of the famous Route 66 from Chicago to Los Angeles. It was first published in 1946, less than a year after the end of World War II. You can use it to retrace the Mother Road as it was at its peak.

U.S. Highway 66 was born around 1926 when a national organization of highway authorities assigned numbers to roads. It went out of official existence on June 27, 1985, when the same group decertified the number. At its birth, the route merely linked a chain of existing roads between towns. As the years passed, new sections were built that shortened the route by eliminating loops.

During World War II, I realized that there might be a great postwar migration from the eastern states to California. Many young men and women had received their war training at the great bases in California, and once having seen that pleasant land they would want to return.

I was not the first writer to see a possible postwar boom in western travel. In 1866, Edward H. Hall wrote his guidebook "The Great West" because be believed the end of the Civil War would "swell the tide of immigration setting into the Eldorado of the West." He gave mileages from Chicago to Rolla, Missouri, and across much of the Southwest.

I knew that most easterners had serious worries about crossing the mountains and deserts. I had made several runs over the route, so I dug into the research needed to do a proper guidebook. Then in March 1946 I made a last, careful round trip to double-check my facts.

That trip was made in a 1939 American Bantam coupe. It was one of the few midget autos made in America: 1200 lbs. curb weight, 75 inch wheelbase, no trunk, no trip odometer, no radio. Its 22 horsepower engine could make 250 miles on the five gallon tank. It sold new for $335.

On that final trip I had to inspect the scenery, so I drove from dawn to dusk at 35 miles an hour. There were no tape recorders then, so I scrawled notes on a big yellow pad on the seat beside me. Each night I dug out my portable manual typewriter and typed my notes.

I made some errors in language. I became so enthused over New Mexico that in one place the text refers to the Gulf of NEW Mexico. And, like many new authors, I wrote about the Rio Grande River, using the redundant wording that is permitted once but not twice to a writer. It was my first book; I was just past thirty-three years old.

We printed 3,000 copies and sold them for a dollar each, doing business by mail to bookshops, newsstands, cafes, and tourist courts (no one then called them motels) along US 66. And I learned the hard way that a self-publishing author usually has a fool for a distributor. I never reached my full market.

Reviewers ignored the little book, but Duncan Hines, who was best known for his restaurant guide, wrote me a nice letter praising the book because it would help people actually see the countryside, not just zip through it. Now, as with the old US 66 signs, that first edition has soared in price as a collector's prize.

So keep this book as your own souvenir, or use it as you try to retrace the old road. Happy traveling!

Jack D. Rittenhouse

Albuquerque, 1988

A GUIDE BOOK
TO HIGHWAY 66

By

JACK D. RITTENHOUSE

PUBLISHED BY
JACK D. RITTENHOUSE

CHAPTER I
HOW TO GET THE MOST FROM THIS BOOK

IMPORTANT! DON'T FAIL TO READ THESE INSTRUC-TIONS FIRST! This Guide Book is not an ordinary trave-logue. It contains many helpful features included because other motorists traveling over US Highway 66 found them useful. You don't start your car in high gear—don't "jump the gun" by skipping this chapter.

MILEAGE FIGURES. Opposite each important entry are two mileage figures, given to the nearest full mile. The first figure, shown in "bold face" (heavy) type, is for the westbound driver. The light face figure (in parentheses) is for the eastbound driver. Follow the figures applying to your direction and the opposite set will show you how far you still have to travel to reach the end of the trip section.

Driving west, you follow the book normally from front to back; traveling east, you must use the book from back to front. It will work equally well either way. The letters (L) or (R) shown in the text in parentheses indicate that the locality indicated is to the left or right from the viewpoint of a westbound driver.

Most travelogues give mileage figures from some central point in a town, such as the city hall. Since the average driver seldom goes to such a central point to start his trip, mileage entries in this book start at some intersection, bridge or noticeable point at the edge of town. Similarly, mileage figures end at the approaches to the large town at the end of each trip section. This allows the tourist to follow any desired route through town and still keep his mileage record straight.

TRIP SECTIONS. For convenience, the entire route has been divided into nine sections, corresponding roughly to

3

the "jumps" made by the average motorist. This is also an aid to the motorist who does not travel the entire distance from Chicago to Los Angeles, but who enters or leaves US 66 at some intermediate point.

At the start of each trip section, opposite the first "0 mi." entry, mark your speedometer's reading in the margin of the page. As you travel, you can then ascertain your location at any time by adding the mileage entry in this book to your own speedometer reading. If your speedometer has a "trip" dial which you can set, this is best, but most late cars no longer have this useful device. Remember, however, that all speedometers differ slightly, and it may be necessary to correct your record from time to time. Follow these instructions carefully, and after traveling a few miles you will find this Guide Book easy to use.

DATA ON TOWNS. Wherever the information could be secured from official sources, the altitude and 1940 population figures for each town have been included. In most towns, at least one garage is listed by name. This is merely to inform you (a) that a garage exists in that town, and (b) to enable you to telephone a garage in case of emergency. **This is not an endorsement or guarantee** of these garages or their work. However, most of the better garages have been included, according to local reputation.

In the description of nearly all towns, some information is included on the facilities available. Motorists want to know if there are cafes, stores, gas stations, hotels, tourist courts, trailer camps, etc., available. To some extent, this can be judged by the population figures: the larger the town, the more complete are its accommodations. In smaller towns, the facilities available are specifically described, and any omission in the description generally indicates a lack of the facility in the town described.

LARGE CITIES. The major cities on US 66 are: Chicago, Springfield, Ill.; Saint Louis; Springfield, Mo.; Joplin, Mo.; Tulsa, Okla.; Oklahoma City; Amarillo, Texas; Albuquerque, New Mexico; and Los Angeles. On each of these metropolitan centers, a separate guide book larger than this could be published. This Guide Book is primarily a guide to the regions **between** large centers. Hence only the salient facts about these large cities are given. If you plan a stay in any of these centers, any major gas station can supply you with a large map of the city, and the Chamber of Commerce will furnish local folders on points of interest.

LODGINGS. It would be ideal if each tourist court and hotel could be listed in detail, with its size, rates, type of accommodations, and rating of quality. However, in view of the unsettled condition in this immediate post-war period, any such detailed listing might change quickly. Furthermore, such listings should be complete and impartial. Perhaps in the next edition, such complete data can be included. In the meantime, the best that can be done is to give a good indication regarding such accommodations.

In spite of the housing shortage, there are still accommodations for tourists—if you do not wait until too late in the day to secure lodgings. The best idea is to plan to stop before 6:00 P. M., earlier if possible, and locate lodgings promptly. Don't wait until after the evening meal—get your cabin or hotel room first, then eat.

ROAD CONDITIONS. The entire highway from Chicago to Los Angeles is well paved and passable. War-worn stretches of pavement are being repaired wherever pitted. Snow comes early and lingers late in stretches between Amarillo, Texas, and Kingman, Arizona, so inquire about road conditions ahead at gas stations when driving during November through March. In case of snow, plows clear the road quickly, but ice on mountain grades is a problem at night.

A FEW SMALL TIPS WHICH MEAN BIG COMFORTS

DON'T WORRY! A trip is no fun if worry sits at the wheel, even if this worry is not voiced to others in the car. So—first of all—rest assured that you're not going to be "hung up" in some forsaken spot. You'll never be more than a score of miles from gas, even in the most desolate areas. There are no impossible grades.

CHECK YOUR EQUIPMENT. Be sure you have your auto jack. A short piece of wide, flat board on which to rest the jack in sandy soil is a sweat-preventer. Include a steel tow-rope, tire tools, tire patches, tire pump, and tire chains. Carry a spare gallon of gas and spare water in the desert areas. Throw a can or two of motor oil in the rear compartment, too. One of those war-surplus foxhole shovels takes little space and may come in very handy. Put new batteries and a new bulb in your flashlight.

Carry a container of drinking water, which becomes a vital necessity as you enter the deserts. For chilly nights and early mornings, you'll find a camp blanket or auto robe useful—and it comes in handy if you find inadequate bedding in a tourist cabin. Don't forget sunglasses for each member of the party. An auto altimeter and auto compass add to the fun of driving, although they are not essential.

You probably won't use all of this stuff, but an hour spent in assembling it before you leave will give you peace of mind, and may save you half a day of discomfort if something **does** happen. Hardly a month goes by that some motorist does not die who would have lived if he had such equipment.

DOCUMENTS. Be sure you have your driver's license, and it is also wise to carry proof of ownership of your car. If you plan to make a side trip into Canada or Mexico, you'll need some evidence of U. S. citizenship: birth certificate, draft registration card, or similar proof.

It is not advisable to carry firearms on tourist trips.

MOUNTAIN AND DESERT DRIVING. On long mountain grades, don't attempt to climb everything in high; shift gears, and shift in plenty of time. Going downgrade, don't coast in neutral, but keep your car in gear, and it won't get out of control. It is assumed that you have adequate brakes, lights, license plates, and a good windshield wiper.

You won't find any desert stretches which are blistered with unendurable heat. Worst stretch is the Mojave Desert, 200 miles of territory running west from the California-Arizona line. In summer months, it is advisable to drive this stretch in the early morning hours or after sundown. Check your oil and water frequently in desert stretches.

When your motor acts oddly at altitudes above 5,000 feet, it may be due to carburetion. In high altitudes, not as much oxygen is contained in the air drawn in, hence the combustion mixture is affected. Cars in high altitude regions usually have special "jets," it is stated. You will find that your car will still operate, however, and the trouble will soon pass as you descend.

DINING EN ROUTE. East of the Mississippi there are many excellent cafes, even in the small towns. This is not the general rule along western cross-country highways, although occasionally very excellent food is obtainable. Many roadside "cafes" serve only chili, sandwiches, pie, coffee, etc. Other establishments bearing a "cafe" sign may be chiefly devoted to the sale of beer or liquor.

TABLE OF DISTANCES

	To Los Angeles	To Chicago
Chicago	2295	0
Bloomington	2155	140
Springfield	2058	237
Saint Louis	1957	338
Rolla	1843	452
Lebanon	1776	519
Springfield (Mo.)	1720	575
Carthage	1661	634
Joplin	1643	652
Miami	1613	682
Claremore	1542	753
Tulsa	1513	782
Oklahoma City	1392	903
Elk City	1276	1019
Shamrock	1222	1073
Amarillo	1130	1165
Tucumcari	1017	1278
Santa Rosa	955	1340
Albuquerque	840	1455
Grants	762	1533
Gallup	695	1600
Holbrook	601	1694
Winslow	568	1727
Flagstaff	507	1788
Williams	473	1822
Ashfork	455	1840
Seligman	431	1864
Kingman	350	1945
Needles	279	2016
Barstow	135	2160
San Bernardino	57	2238
Los Angeles	0	2295

Well, you're on your way—over two thousand miles of fascinating highway ahead of you. One of life's biggest thrills is the realization that "we're on the way," which the motorist feels as he eases the car away from the curb and heads out of town.

Since you may leave Chicago from some neighborhood removed from the center of town, wait until you've reached the town of Plainfield before noting your first speedometer reading. Plainfield is only about 35 miles from the center of Chicago.

 In leaving Chicago on US 66, you will find the route plainly marked through city streets, running southwest from the Loop district. About 25 miles from the City Hall, you will reach a fork in the road, where main US 66 goes ahead to Plainfield and alternate US 66 forks left to Joliet. You may take the Joliet road, if you wish, since the main and alternate highways join again farther south. However, since this Guide Book covers only main—not alternate —routes, we assume you continue on US 66 to Plainfield, about 10 miles from the fork.

In the center of Plainfield there is an intersection of US 66 with east-west US 30, and the stoplight at this intersection is the starting point. Mark your speedometer reading in the margin of this page at this point. And if you have not already read Chapter I, go back and read it now, so you will understand the system of mileage records, data listed on towns, etc.

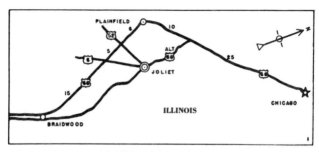

0 mi. (264 mi.) **PLAINFIELD.** (Pop. 1,485. Gas; stores; Ferd's Motor Sales Garage.)

Leaving Plainfield, you will find yourself on an Illinois "freeway"—one of a series of new super-highways being constructed under terms of an act passed in 1943. From Chicago to St. Louis, this road—when completed—will be a wide, improved highway which will allow speed and safety by skirting all smaller towns, and by restrictions against operating gas stations, cafes, courts, etc., directly on the highway. To reach such accommodations, you will have to turn off the highway a few hundred yards or less.

6 mi. (240 mi.) Junction with US 52. Gas; cafes. Five miles farther, at a grade separation, is the junction with US 6, running east to Joliet.

14 mi. (232 mi.) Cross the Desplaines River on a steel bridge. For the next four miles (L) you pass the site of the Kankakee Plant of the Joliet Arsenal, active during World War II. At **19 mi.** (227 mi.) you cross the Kankakee River.

21 mi. (225 mi.) Gas station. Another gas station with a cafe and a few cabins at **22 mi.** (224 mi.)

As you approach **BRAIDWOOD** (Pop. 1,354; alt. 581';

stores; gas; cafes) at **26 mi.** (220 mi.), you pass between huge heaps of dirt and "slag"—refuse from the coal pits which made this a boom area at one time. In Braidwood is the famous Peter Rossi macaroni plant, originally founded in 1876 and still operating in what appear to be the original buildings. Leaving Braidwood, you pass a few tourist cabins (R) and some old mine structures (L).

29 mi. (217 mi.) **GODLEY.** (Pop. 85; no facilities.) Once a booming mining community. Now only a few homes remain. South of the town are more slag heaps.

30 mi. (216 mi.) **BRACEVILLE.** (Pop. 321; alt. 583'; few gas stations; cafes; small garage.) Like Godley, this town is but a remnant of a once-thriving coal town. As you leave town, the typical slag-heaps still blot the countryside.

34 mi. (212 mi.) The town of **GARDNER** lies to the east of US 66 here. (Pop. 864; alt. 590'; garage.) There are gas stations and a cafe on US 66 at this intersection. This community now depends on the surrounding farms for its existence.

36 mi. (210 mi.) Enter **DWIGHT.** (Pop. 2,499; alt. 657'; few tourist cabins; small hotels; Boyer Bros. Garage; stores.) A large veterans' hospital is located in Dwight, but it is perhaps best known as the home of the famous **KEELEY INSTITUTE**, which has treated almost a half-million persons for alcoholism and drug addiction. The institute (which you may visit) was founded after the Civil War by Dr. Leslie Keeley, whose cure is based on the principle that alcoholism is a definite disease. The town of Dwight is quiet and pleasant.

44 mi. (202 mi.) The town of **ODELL,** as in the similar case of Dwight, lies east of US 66 at this point. (Pop. 927;

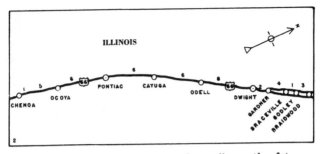

alt. 721′; garage, etc., in town.) One mile south of town, there is a gas station on the highway.

50 mi. (196 mi.) **CAYUGA.** (Alt. 696′) A grain elevator, a small school, one store, and a dozen homes comprise this community. No gas station or other facilities here.

56 mi. (190 mi.) **PONTIAC** is a half-mile east of US 66 at this point. (Pop. 9,585; alt. 645′; gas; stores; no cabins; hotels: Phoenix, Maple Rest, Imperial, Illinois; Jones Co. garage.) By now you are well out of the northern Illinois coal-mining district, and Pontiac is an active community dependent primarily on agriculture but also having some industrial plants and railroad activity. The town is over a hundred years old, and is named for a famous Indian chief. One mile south of the town are the buildings (L) of a branch of the **STATE PENITENTIARY**, where younger male criminals are detained.

At **58 mi.** (188 mi.) a neat modernistic building houses a district headquarters of the Illinois State Police (R). At **59 mi.** (187 mi.) are the red brick buildings (R) of the Livingston County Home along the roadside.

62 mi. (184 mi.) **OCOYA**, another dwindling community with the ever-present grain elevator, a score of homes, two small stores and a gas station, lies just off US 66 (L) here.

67 mi. (179 mi.) **CHENOA.** (Pop. 1,401; alt. 722'; Burch & Downe's garage; several cafes and gas stations; few cabins.) Town is a few hundred yards (L) off US 66. Junction here with US 24. Pike Hotel in Chenoa.

76 mi. (170 mi.) **LEXINGTON.** (Pop. 1,284; alt. 746'; small business district with gas stations, etc., garage, but no hotel.) One of the earlier communities settled in this region, it was named after the famous Massachusetts town. The new freeway, by skirting these smaller towns, is affecting the portion of their income formerly received from tourists.

84 mi. (162 mi.) **TOWANDA.** (Pop. 430; alt. 787'; garage; stores.) A small business district is off the highway (R).

95 mi. (151 mi.) **NORMAL** and **BLOOMINGTON.** These two towns are virtually one community, with their city limits adjoining along one side. US 66 skirts both towns completely, with a road west to the cities at the mileage point given.

Illinois State Normal University is located in **NORMAL** (Pop. 6,983; alt. 790'; stores; hotels; Broadway Garage).

BLOOMINGTON (Pop. 32,868; alt. 853'; stores; Wanne-macher's garage and Cherry St. Garage) is the birthplace of Elbert Hubbard, and is the city in which the Illinois Republican Party was organized at a convention in 1856, at which Lincoln spoke. Hotels here include the Illinois, Rogers, Hamilton, Tilden Hall, Phoenix, Commercial. Radio station WJBC—1230 kilocycles.

97 mi. (149 mi.) **SHIRLEY** (Pop. 133; alt. 765'; garage.)

No tourist facilities in this small community, with its grain elevators surrounded by smaller cribs to hold extra grain. A few homes and a few stores.

101 mi. (145 mi.) **FUNK'S GROVE** (Pop. 46; alt. 697'; gas station; cafe; no tourist accommodations). The town itself lies across the railroad tracks which parallel US 66 (R).

107 mi. (139 mi.) **McLEAN** (Pop. 652; alt. 711'; Van Ness Garage). Another small community, but it provides a gas station and cafe.

112 mi. (134 mi.) **ATLANTA** (Pop. 1,290; alt. 722'; garage; gas; cafes; no cabins or hotel). US 66 goes down one of the main business streets, past some very old store buildings, some dating back to the 1850's.

116 mi. (130 mi.) **LAWNDALE.** Really not a town at all, since it consists of a couple of red railroad shacks, a few homes, and a pair of grain elevators. No facilities at all on US 66.

122 mi. (124 mi.) Nearing **LINCOLN** (Pop. 12,752; alt. 590'; stores; Hoelscher Bros. garage and Sheer garage; hotels include: Western, Commercial, Lincoln; Elm Grove Court). Main US 66 straight ahead, city route forks left. At a junction with Illinois Road 10, just north of Lincoln, are gas stations and cafes.

Entering Lincoln, you pass the Logan County Fair Grounds (L) where the fair is usually held in early August. The city of Lincoln was named for Abraham Lincoln after he prepared legal documents for the original promoters of the townsite. Lincoln practiced law here in the late 1850's, but the courthouse in which he spoke has been rebuilt.

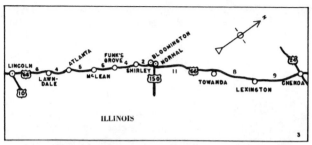

ILLINOIS

At the south edge of Lincoln, City Route 66 comes in from the left to rejoin the main route. **126 mi.** (120 mi.)

132 mi. (114 mi.) **BROADWELL** (Pop. 144; alt. 594'; gas; grocery; cafe; no garage). Two-score homes surround a tiny depot and the grain elevators which bear witness to the corn growing ability of this region.

136 mi. (110 mi.) **ELKHART** (Pop. 436; alt. 594'; garage; gas.) The dozen ancient store buildings which comprise the town are off to the left on the one main street which crosses US 66. No courts here.

143 mi. (103 mi.) **WILLIAMSVILLE** (Pop. 649; alt. 604'). The town is a quarter of a mile off US 66 (L). There is a garage in the town, but no gas station or other facilities on the highway.

147 mi. (99 mi.) **SHERMAN** (Pop. 100; alt. 579'; gas; Withrow garage; grocery). Here begins a 5-mile stretch of divided highway, which you frequently encounter along US 66 in Illinois where the new freeway is being completed.

149 mi. (97 mi.) Cross the **SANGAMON RIVER,** and begin to enter the outskirts of **SPRINGFIELD.** The main route of US 66 passes through town, near the business district, and is usually taken by tourists who wish to visit the

15

Lincoln historical spots. On the north side of town, you pass the Fair Grounds (R), about 3 miles from the center of town.

SPRINGFIELD (Pop. 75,503; alt. 644'; radio stations WCBS, 1450 kc., and WTAX, 1240 kc.; garages: Uptown, Thomas, Motor Inn, Midtown, and others; main hotels include: Abraham Lincoln, Leland, St. Nicholas, and Illinois. Courts include: Highway Hotel Ct., Bedini's Lakeview Cabins, Johnny & Janey Camp, Ahrenkiel Service Station Camp, Capitol Tourist Camp, Moderne Ct., Poland's Modern Ctgs., and Sabattini's Cabins. A good cafe is Maldaner's.)

Springfield is famous as the home of Abraham Lincoln from 1837 until he left for Washington in 1861. His home, located in the center of the town (watch for markers on US 66), is open to visitors (free). The Lincoln Tomb is also in Springfield, together with sites of many other historic Lincoln events. Other points of interest include state capitol buildings, historical museums and libraries, etc. The State Museum houses mineralogical and other exhibits. Vachel Lindsay, poet, was a long-time resident here. The Illinois State Fair is held here the last part of August. Any local resident can direct you to points of interest.

Leaving Springfield, By-pass 66 comes in from the left at **159 mi.** (87 mi.), and a short distance south is the large Springfield plant of the Allis-Chalmers Co. At **160 mi.** (86 mi.) is the entrance to **LINCOLN ORDNANCE DEPOT**, and soon after, you cross **LAKE SPRINGFIELD**, with its bathing beaches. At **163 mi.** (83 mi.) is a road (L) to **LINCOLN NATIONAL MEMORIAL GARDENS**.

16

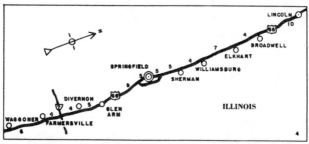

168 mi. (78 mi.) **GLEN ARM.** A dozen homes comprise this community, with a few gas stations, stores, cafe, Atchison's Garage. At **171 mi.** (75 mi.), at the junction with state road 104, are gas stations and a cafe.

173 mi. (73 mi.) **SUNDOWN CORNER,** at a junction with a road to **DIVERNON,** a half-mile west. Gas station at intersection. Divernon (Pop. 1,033, alt. 614′) is a small, quiet town. Garage here.

177 mi. (69 mi.) Junction with road 7 mi. west to **VIRDEN.** Gas station and grocery with 3 cabins. Another gas station, cafe, and 8 cabins is a few hundred yards north.

Virden was the scene of historic coal strikes in the 90's. In 1898, there was a battle between strikers and company guards in which 10 miners and guards were killed.

180 mi. (66 mi.) Gas station. At **181 mi.** (65 mi.), US 66 barely touches the eastern edge of the town of **FARMERS-VILLE** (Pop. 550; gas; cafes; Cundiff garage).

186 mi. (60 mi.) Gas station. The town of **WAGGONER** is about a half-mile west of here. At **191 mi.** (55 mi.) is a gas station, cafe, and 5 tourist cabins, with a First Aid Station.

194 mi. (52 mi.) Gas here at junction with state road 108.

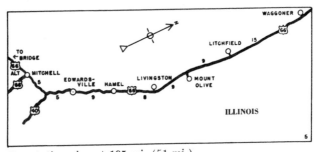

Gas station also at **195 mi.** (51 mi.)

201 mi. (45 mi.) Right here a short distance to town of
LITCHFIELD (Pop. 7,048; alt. 687′; gas; cafes; few tourist cabins; garages: Hittmeier Bros. and Oldsmobile;
hotel). This is an old mining town, and was also the locale
of early oil production.

209 mi. (37 mi.) Gas station.

210 mi. (36 mi.) Intersection with a graveled road (L),
leading to **MOUNT OLIVE.** A few roadside tables at this
intersection. A few hundred yards off (L) on this graveled
road is the **MOUNT OLIVE UNION MINERS CEME-
TERY,** where members of the coal unions bury their dead.
Here there is a monument over the grave of "Mother"
Jones, a famous woman leader of the miners who died in
1930 at the age of 100.

MOUNT OLIVE (Pop. 2,559; alt. 677′; garage; gas; small
hotel). A small mining and farming town.

214 mi. (32 mi.) Here there is a side road off (R) at a
tangent, leading to **LITCHFIELD.** At the intersection is
the 66 Tourist Camp with cabins, gas, etc.

217 mi. (29 mi.) West a half-mile and visible from the

road, are the workings of the Mount Olive and Stanton Coal Co.

219 mi. (27 mi.) US 66 barely touches the eastern edge of **LIVINGSTON** (Pop. 1,115). Gas station on highway.

223 mi. (23 mi.) Junction with a road (R) to STAUNTON. A truckers' stop is at the junction, with gas and cafes and a few cabins. At **224 mi.** (22 mi.) is Nelson's Tourist Court, with a gas station.

227 mi. (19 mi.) **HAMEL** (Pop. 160), a small farming community with several implement stores. Hamel Service Co. garage. No cabins or other accommodations, except gas.

230 mi. (16 mi.) Green Gables tourist court and gas station. Another gas station at **232 mi.** (14 mi.)

236 mi. (10 mi.) **EDWARDSVILLE.** (Pop. 8,008; alt. 452'; Bothman garage; hotels: Leland, Colonial; homes offer rooms for tourists; gas; cafes.) This is an old town dating back to shortly after the War of 1812. Several Indian and pioneer relics are on display in a county historical museum here.

241 mi. (5 mi.) Here US 66 curves and drops down a slight hill into the Mississippi River bottom lands. Near the foot of the hill (L) is the Sunset Hill Coal Mine, and at the foot of the hill is a junction with US 40 (Bypass). A picnic spot with tables is at the junction, by a gas station.

244 mi. (2 mi.) Junction with state road 111. Gas station, cafe and garage here.

246 mi. (0 mi.) **MITCHELL.** (Alt. 432'; Paul's Garage; gas stations, cafe; no cabins.) Here City Route 66 forks off to the left into Saint Louis, while main US 66 crosses railroad tracks and continues ahead to the **CHAIN OF ROCKS BRIDGE** and the "belt line" route skirting the city. Going west, end your mileage records here, and start them again on the west edge of Saint Louis. Driving east, note your speedometer reading in the margin here, to follow readings from here to Chicago.

If you are taking the route around Saint Louis, continue straight ahead five miles to the **CHAIN OF ROCKS TOLL BRIDGE** across the **MISSISSIPPI RIVER**. (Tolls: auto and occupants—25c.)

If you are not planning to stop in St. Louis, your best route is to follow US 66 across the Chain of Rocks Bridge and around the city. US 66 passes the north edge of the city, turns south near the Airport, continues down the west side of the city, through Kirkwood, Mo., and rejoins City 66 at a point 26 miles from Chain of Rocks Bridge. This "belt line" is a wide, high-speed route, with plenty of gas stations and a few tourist cabins and cafes. It avoids city traffic completely.

SAINT LOUIS (Pop. 816,048; alt. 445'; radio stations: KMOX—1120 kc., KSD—550 kc., KXOX—630 kc., KWK—1380 kc.; several auto courts on western approach over US 66; 22 major hotels; all accommodations.) The eighth largest city in the U. S., it offers many sights: Municipal Opera, Zoo, Art Museum, major league baseball, Washington University, parks, Jefferson Memorial, etc.

One of the best courts is **King Brothers Motel, on** "belt line" 66 where Lindbergh Road meets Clayton. Other courts on west side of town are Wayside, 66, and Bluebonnet. Hotels include: Statler, Chase, York, DeSoto, Coronado, Jefferson, Mayfair, Melbourne, Park Plaza.

CHAPTER III
SAINT LOUIS, MISSOURI, TO SPRINGFIELD, MISSOURI

This section of your journey takes you through the colorful Ozark country, with its hills, old villages, swift streams and deep caves. Your first speedometer reading is at a

 "cloverleaf" intersection on the west side of Saint Louis, where City 66 meets Bypass 66. If you have driven over Bypass 66, you will make a right turn at this intersection 2 miles south of **KIRKWOOD.**

If you have driven through the center of St. Louis, you can follow City 66 from the center of town, over Gravois Ave., Chippewa St., and Watson Road. City 66 meets the above-mentioned intersection about 13 miles from the City Hall in the center of St. Louis.

0 mi. (221 mi.) Intersection of City 66 and Bypass 66. Mark your speedometer reading in the margin of this page. If starting your trip at this point, read Chapter I.

Along US 66 for several miles west of St. Louis, you pass the **HENRY SHAW GARDEN WAY,** a section planted along the highway to display native trees, shrubs and plants.

2 mi. (219 mi.) **SYLVAN BEACH,** on the Meramec River, is a popular resort. You will cross the Meramec again at **13 mi.** (208 mi.). The highway between these two localities is a pretty, semi-rural route, well-paved.

15 mi. (206 mi.) **EUREKA.** (Pop. 663; alt. 465′; gas.) A

21

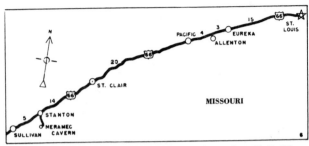

small community established just before the Civil War.

18 mi. (203 mi.) **ALLENTON** (Pop. 301; alt. 480';) is a small community across the railroad tracks (L). It offers no tourist facilities on US 66.

21 mi. (200 mi.) A **HISTORICAL MARKER** beside the highway here (L) states this point was reached by the Confederate Army in 1864. On the other side of the highway is a high bluff, with a **SCENIC OVERLOOK** at its summit, reached by a stairway. Parking space at foot of bluff.

22 mi. (199 mi.) **PACIFIC.** (Pop. 1,687; alt. 466'; gas; garage; stores.) At the eastern edge of town is the Pioneer Silica Products Co. mine, typical of the mines here which produce silica for fine glassware.

26 mi. (195 mi.) The village of Gray Summit is off to the right here, and US 66 crosses a deep cut through which a railroad runs. Watch for the tunnel (R).

27 mi. (194 mi.) **TRUCK WEIGHING STATION** here (R).

34 mi. (187 mi.) US 66 crosses the **BOURBEUSE RIVER** here on a double bridge. From here into St. Louis, US 66 has three or more lanes.

40 mi. (181 mi.) Gas station. From here into St. Louis, there are plenty of gas stations and cafes.

42 mi. (179 mi.) SAINT CLAIR. (Pop. 1,410; alt. 769'; gas; garage; Commercial Hotel; Johnson's Mo-Tel.) US 66 passes town on the west edge. Over 100 years old, it is a peaceful town, full of sedate old residences.

47 mi. (174 mi.) Hobbyists who collect minerals will be interested in a large shop by the roadside here, selling specimens of minerals from Missouri.

49 mi. (172 mi.) Gas station and cafe here. Benson's Tourist City, an elaborate establishment with cabins, cafe, gas, and trailer camp, is at **50 mi.** (171 mi.). Another gas station, with a cafe and a few tourist cabins, is at **51 mi.** (170 mi.).

In this part of Missouri, US 66 winds through rich farm country. The low hills are the beginnings of the Ozarks with outcroppings of clay and limestone.

54 mi. (167 mi.) STANTON. (Pop. 115; alt. 872'; Stanton garage; AAA garage; gas; cafe; store; few cabins.) A good cafe here is Wurzburger's (L). A few miles (L) from here on a well-marked road, to **MERAMEC CAVERN** (admission charged). This is a remarkable cave, one of the most popular in Missouri, and worth visiting. The last few hundred yards of the road leading to the Cavern are winding and drop down a short grade into the Meramec River gorge.

59 mi. (162 mi.) SULLIVAN. (Pop. 2,517; alt. 977'; Campbell Chevrolet Co. garage; Grande Courts; Sullmo Cabins; cafes.) The main business district of the town is off US 66, which touches the western edge of town. Just north of Sullivan is the entrance (L) to **MERAMEC STATE PARK**, one of the best public recreational areas in the state, including over 7,000 acres of woodland, equipped with trails, cabins, bathing beach, etc. A cave is located in the Park, with guides to direct sightseers. (Small admission charge to cave.)

67 mi. (154 mi.) **BOURBON** (Pop. 360; alt. 954′; Roede-meier garage; few cabins; gas; cafes) is a smaller village, with its business district a few blocks off US 66 (L).

69 mi. (152 mi.) Gas station. At **71 mi.** (150 mi.) is a road (L) to **ONONDAGA CAVE**, another of the most popular caverns in Missouri. (Admission charged; guides.) A deep, mysterious cavern, with an underground river, "rooms" of striking onyx formations and other unusual features. At the intersection of this side road with US 66 are a gas station and two inns.

75 mi. (146 mi.) **HOFFLINS** (Pop. 48) is truly a small town; one store and one home, but it has a post office.

78 mi. (143 mi.) **CUBA.** (Pop. 1,033; alt. 1,000′; garages: Souder's and Square Deal; hotels: New Central and Cuba; cabin courts: Wagon Wheel, Barnsdall, Red Horse Tavern.) Although still important as an agricultural center, Cuba is now an important highway town.

83 mi. (138 mi.) **FANNING** (Pop. 59; alt. 1,059′; gas station but no other facilities) is a town which the new US 66 almost missed, the new road almost cutting off the one store and meeting hall which comprise the community.

85 mi. (136 mi.) An Ozark basket and curio store is located here, selling native handicraft articles. You will find several such along US 66 in the Ozarks. There is a gas station with a few cabins at **88 mi.** (133 mi.) and another at **90 mi.** (131 mi.).

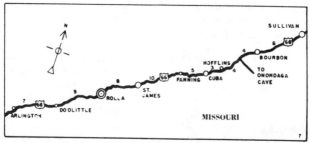

93 mi. (128 mi.) **SAINT JAMES.** (Pop. 1,812; alt. 1,087′; garage; hospital; gas; cafes; courts: American Way and Kozy Kottage.) A Federal Soldiers Home is maintained here. The town holds a grape festival each September. This is the last community on the "plains"; soon you enter the Ozarks.

101 mi. (120 mi.) Enter outskirts of **ROLLA.** (Pop. 5,141; alt. 1,092′; major hotels: Edwin Long and Sinclair Pennant; courts: Colonial Village; Phelps', Schuman's Tourist City, El Caney, Trav-L-Odge, Winter's; Vance Motor Co. garage; all facilities.) Rolla is the locale of the **MISSOURI SCHOOL OF MINES,** whose buildings you pass if you take City 66 instead of main US 66 around the business district. The school maintains an extensive mineral exhibit. Federal troops used Rolla as a headquarters in the Civil War. The town holds an Ozark Folk Festival in May. As you leave town, you pass a **TRACHOMA HOSPITAL** (R).

106 mi. (115 mi.) **MARTIN'S SPRINGS,** a large flowing spring typical of many found in the Ozarks, is housed here (L) in a low stone building beside the highway.

108 mi. (113 mi.) Gas station. At **110 mi.** (111 mi.) you enter **DOOLITTLE,** a community loosely strung along about two miles of highway. (Pop. 208; Five-Oaks garage; gas; few cabins; cafe.)

115 mi. (106 mi.) Totem Pole Cabins, built of logs. Just north of here is a roadside park (R) with wooden tables. Gas station at **116 mi.** (105 mi.).

117 mi. (104 mi.) **ARLINGTON.** (Pop. 40; alt. 689'; no gas or other facilities.) Arlington is a small, old-style village whose main street was cut off by a new highway. In 1946, the buildings of the town were sold for $10,000 to Rowe Carney, of Rolla, who intends to develop it as a resort. It nestles on the bank of the Little Piney River.

118 mi. (103 mi.) **STONY DELL**, a popular Ozark resort, has several stone buildings, including a gas station and the office of its Justice of the Peace. Store and several cabins, also a swimming pool. Leaving here, you start up a grade about one mile long—one of a dozen such grades you will encounter in the Ozarks.

120 mi. (101 mi.) Cafe and a few cabins. Through the Ozarks, you will find many small tourist camps. These establishments were not built for the cross-country tourist as much as for the week-end tourists from Saint Louis, for whom the Ozarks is a great playground. Fishermen come to the region from the Midwest. Hence, accommodations at times may be a little more Spartan than the deluxe courts for tourists usually found.

121 mi. (100 mi.) **POWELLVILLE.** A gas station, cafe, and a few cabins.

122 mi. (99 mi.) **CLEMENTINE.** Hardly a town, but chiefly devoted to small roadside stands selling handmade hickory baskets and turned wood objects made by native craftsmen. The stands here are among the best of their type in the Ozarks.

You now enter a stretch of divided highway, built during

World War II to facilitate traffic to Fort Leonard Wood, which is nearby. The road is an engineering triumph and truly a joy to the traveler.

124 mi. (97 mi.) **HOOKER.** (Pop. 120; alt. 710'; gas; no other accommodations.) Before the new highway was built, the road went past an odd geological formation known as **DEVIL'S ELBOW.** If you are interested in seeing this, you can take a fork off US 66 from Hooker.

125 mi. (96 mi.) Gas station, near the foot of a grade rising for the next mile.

131 mi. (90 mi.) A Missouri State Patrol station is located  here, with its radio tower in the grassy plot between the divided highway. Gas stations here also, and nearby is the entrance (L) to **FORT LEONARD WOOD**, site of a large training center during World War II.

Between Ft. Leonard Wood and Waynesville, 4 miles farther, there are several cafes, bars, gas stations, cabins, etc., built during the War. At **133 mi.** (88 mi.) the divided highway ends, and US 66 goes down a fairly steep grade into Waynesville.

WAYNESVILLE. (Pop. 468 in 1940, much higher now; alt. 800'; garages: C. C., Bell, OK; cafes; stores; Bell Hotel; few cabins.) During the war, Waynesville was the chief recreational center for the soldiers from Ft. Leonard Wood. It experienced a sudden boom, which is only gradually declining. Leave town at **135 mi.** (86 mi.).

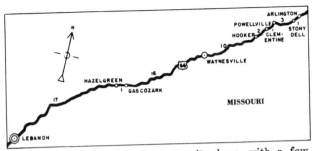

140 mi. (81 mi.) A small community here, with a few homes, gas stations, Bowden garage, and cafe. During the Civil War, most of this region was Southern in sentiment.

141 mi. (80 mi.) Gas stations and a cafe here. You are now in the **MARK TWAIN NATIONAL FOREST**, and entering one of the most beautiful sections of the Ozarks. At **142 mi.** (79 mi.) are some roadside picnic tables (L) among the trees.

There are gas stations at **143 mi.** (78 mi.), **147 mi.** (74 mi.), and **149 mi.** (72 mi.). At **150 mi.** (71 mi.) you reach **GASCOZARK**, a small community consisting of a store and two gas stations.

151 mi. (70 mi.) **HAZELGREEN.** (Pop. 45; gas; store; small hotel.) This town is typical of many throughout the Ozarks, drawing their livelihood from the fishermen and vacationists who throng the region. As in nearby villages, native pottery and other handicraft articles are sold here. Leaving Hazelgreen, you drop down into the valley of the **GASCONADE RIVER**, and climb its southern bank to **EDEN RESORT**, one of the best accommodations in this region. By the roadside (R) are public stone picnic tables.

In this part of the Ozarks, cabin camps are frequent: some fairly good, others quite run down. Most have gas stations.

155 mi. (66 mi.) Cabins and gas. 156 mi. (65 mi.) Lucy's cabins. 159 mi. (62 mi.) Gas. 160 mi. (61 mi.) Gas and cabins. 164 mi. (57 mi.) Vesta Court; gas.

168 mi. (53 mi.) Enter **LEBANON.** (Pop. 5,025; alt. 1,265'; garages; hotels: Harris, Laclede, Nelson; courts: Camp Joy, Nelson Dream Village, Clark's Rock Court, Green Gables; all facilities.) US 66 skirts the eastern edge of the town, which is the major community on US 66 between Rolla and Springfield.

From Lebanon, US 66 runs westward to Springfield, and the highway marks the northern border of the **"OZARKS**  **PLAYGROUND,"** a large region of lake resorts for vacationists and fishermen. It is famous as the locale of "The Shepherd of the Hills," by **HAROLD BELL WRIGHT,** who was for a time pastor of a church in Lebanon. The cabin of Old Matt, a character in the novel, is about 60 miles south of Springfield.

From March through October, the Ozarks are at their best. Nights are cool and starry, the weather pleasant. Winding roads lead off main highways into green retreats and weathered gorges. More than 100 varieties of trees blanket the rolling hills, laced with swift streams down which fishermen may float for days in boats provided by skilled guides. While these attractions also apply to the Ozarks between Lebanon and St. Louis, they reach their richest beauty in the area south of the Lebanon-Springfield stretch of US 66.

170 mi. (51 mi.) Leave **LEBANON.** Because of the many resorts between here and Springfield, you will find a gas station at almost every milestone, many equipped with a

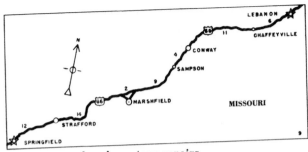

small garage for elementary repairs.

175 mi. (46 mi.) Gas station and cabins. At **176 mi.** (45 mi.) is **CHAFFEYVILLE**, a small hamlet, consisting chiefly of a gas station, cafe, and a few cabins.

177 mi. (44 mi.) Gas and cabins. **181 mi.** (40 mi.) Gas and cabins. **182 mi.** (39 mi.) Gas and cabins. **183 mi.** (38 mi.) Roadside park (L), with tables and fireplaces for picnicking. Gas station nearby.

186 mi. (35 mi.) **CONWAY.** (Pop. 516; alt. 1,406'; gas; garage; cafe; few cabins.) A small business district is off US 66 (L).

188 mi. (33 mi.) Gas station and cafe. **189 mi.** (32 mi.) Gas station. From Lebanon to Springfield, the highway is winding and traverses hilly country.

190 mi. (31 mi.) **SAMPSON.** (Pop. 22; gas; few cabins.) Along the highway in this section there are some old, stubby telephone poles, reminiscent of the Civil War days when the route of what is now US 66 was a trail known as the "Wire Road," because of the military telegraph line which ran along it, several miles north of here.

192 mi. (29 mi.) Gas station and cafe. **194 mi.** (27 mi.)

Abbylee Court and cafe. **196 mi.** (25 mi.) Oak Vale Court, with gas and cafe.

199 mi. (22 mi.) Gas station. Just southwest of here a road forks off (L) to Marshfield. At **201 mi.** (20 mi.) is an intersection of US 66 with the main road into Marshfield.

MARSHFIELD. (Pop. 1,764; alt. 1,491'; Tarr's garage; Webster hotel; stores; few cabins.) The town of Marshfield is a short distance off US 66. At the intersection of US 66 and the road into town, there are several small cafes, gas stations, and a few tourist cabins. The village of Marshfield is a quiet, agricultural community, little touched by the rush of the highway traffic.

In passing, it should be mentioned that many of the "cafes" mentioned in this Guide Book do not serve full-course meals. Often, many roadside cafes serve only sandwiches, soups, chili, pie and similar light food. The size of the cafe building is usually an indication of its menu. Any time you see several huge trucks parked outside a roadside cafe, you can usually be assured of excellent coffee and possibly other food as well, for these men who make long drives know where to stop.

205 mi. (16 mi.) Gas station. Another at **206 mi.** (15 mi.).

207 mi. (14 mi.) Start climbing a one-mile, winding grade. At the top is Red Top tourist camp: cabins and gas.

210 mi. (11 mi.) Oak Grove Lodge: gas and cabins.

215 mi. (6 mi.) Enter **STRAFFORD** (Pop. 311; alt. 1,482'; McDowell garage; gas; no courts), a community whose peak has been passed, now only a suburb of Springfield.

218 mi. (3 mi.) Gas station. Another at **219 mi.** (2 mi.).

221 mi. (0 mi.) Enter northeast edge of **SPRINGFIELD.** (Pop. 61,238; alt. 1,324'; all types of accommodations:) There are two routes: through town on City 66, or around it on Bypass 66. There are plenty of tourist courts on all approaches to the city, and several hotels in town.

Largest hotels are: Colonial, Kentwood Arms, Seville, and Metropolitan; also Milner, State and Sterling Hotels. Tourist courts include: Cordova, Lone Star, Baldridge, Black's, Camp-On-A-Way, Curtis, DeLuxe, Eagle, Lone Pine, Mack's, New Haven, Otto's, Ozark, Rail Haven, Red Bird, Rock Village, Royal, Snow White, Springfield and White Haven.

Radio stations: KGBX—1260 kc., KTTS—1400 kc., KWTO —560 kc.

Springfield is Missouri's fourth largest city, and is a popular tourist and vacationist center—offering excellent hospitality. The Ozark Empire Fair is held here every September. The O'Reilly General Hospital is located here, containing 5,000 beds. The community has over 200 manufacturing plants. The first settler arrived here in 1829, and two years later the first school was built. Both Confederate and Union dead were buried here in the Civil War.

If you are driving straight through in a hurry, take Bypass 66, which runs along the northern edge of the city and then turns south a short distance and again turns west. For a part of the route, US 66 passes through a portion of the city, but for the most part it avoids city traffic. Your speedometer readings were ended at the northeastern approach to Springfield; readings will be resumed at the intersection of Bypass 66 and City 66 on the west side of town, about 10 miles from the northeastern edge of town.

GOING EAST? GOING WEST?

STOP... See Missouri En Route

● The family fun state—Missouri—offering splendid vacation spots quickly reached by scenic highways. You'll be just within shouting distance of your favorite sport. There's fun, room—a rousing welcome for ALL in the Midwest's most popular playground—MISSOURI!

For full color folders and special road map, write: Missouri State Department of Resources and Development, Dept. RM-12, Jefferson City, Missouri.

THE STATE OF MISSOURI
IN THE HEART OF AMERICA

33

CHAPTER IV
SPRINGFIELD, MISSOURI, TO TULSA, OKLAHOMA

The next section of your trip is from Springfield, Mo., to Tulsa, Okla. The hills in this region are lower and less  frequent than in the Ozarks, and the road winds through bandit country, mining districts and cattle ranges. The region is more thickly settled than the Ozarks, and there are more farms.

0 mi. (214 mi.) As you leave **SPRINGFIELD,** you will come to an intersection of City 66 and Bypass 66 at the western edge of town. Note your speedometer reading in the margin of the page at this point. You will have about 4 miles of four-lane highway west of Springfield.

6 mi. (208 mi.) Andy's Court. Next gas station at **8. mi.** (206 mi.). From here to eastern Oklahoma, you will find gas stations plentiful, especially in western Missouri.

9 mi. (205 mi.) A small community here, with a custom grinding mill (L), gas station, grocery and general store.

11 mi. (203 mi.) Gas station and cabins. At **14 mi.** (200 mi.) is Camp Ross Court, with a cafe and gas station, on the bank of Pickerel Creek.

20 mi. (194 mi.) **HALLTOWN.** (Pop. 168; alt. 1,143'.) 15 or 20 establishments line both sides of the highway here: gas stations, cafes, antique shops, stores.

23 mi. (191 mi.) **PARIS SPRINGS JUNCTION.** A small crossroads, providing two gas stations and a grocery.

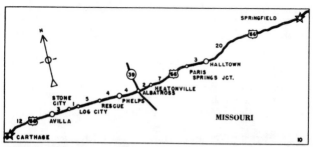

24 mi. (190 mi.) Gas station and grocery, on the bank of Johnson Creek. One mile farther, at **25 mi.** (189 mi.) is Camp Lookout: a few cabins and a gas station. At **26 mi.** (188 mi.) is another gas station and grocery, with a small garage just west of here. Small grocery at **28 mi.** (186 mi.). **30 mi.** (184 mi.) **HEATONVILLE.** Garages, groceries, gas stations, general store and Castle Rock Cabins here.

32 mi. (182 mi.) **ALBATROSS.** At junction of US 66 and State Road 39. Garage, several gas stations, cafes and Carver's Cabins.

36 mi. (178 mi.) **PHELPS.** Gas stations, cafe, a few homes, and two very old store buildings comprise Phelps. No tourist accommodations. Another gas station at **39 mi.** (175 mi.).

40 mi. (174 mi.) **RESCUE.** (Brown's garage; Reed's cabins.) A small village with a few homes and a couple of groceries.

41 mi. (173 mi.) Gas station; also Shadyside Camp. More gas stations at **43 mi.** (171 mi.).

45 mi. (169 mi.) **LOG CITY.** Like **STONE CITY,** which is at **46 mi.** (168 mi.), this is a popular resort with cabins frequented by vacationists for week-ends or longer. Buildings are of stone and logs. Gas stations, store and cafes.

48 mi. (166 mi.) Gas stations and White Oak cabins.

49 mi. (165 mi.) **AVILLA.** (Pop. 178) Gas, cafe, stores. The lumber yard and farm implement stores here indicate its importance as an agricultural trading and supply center.

As you near Carthage, about 13 miles from Avilla, you begin to leave the more wooded sections of the Ozarks, already fairly sparse, and the hills end.

57 mi. (157 mi.) Two gas stations, one with a garage.

59 mi. (155 mi.) A roadside park here (L) on the banks of the lovely, green **Spring River.**

As you approach the edge of Carthage, US 66 forks: City 66 turns left, main US 66 goes straight ahead. City route is shorter and traffic in Carthage is not heavy enough to slow you up.

61 mi. (153 mi.) **CARTHAGE.** (Pop. 10,585; alt. 942′ hotels: Drake, Crane, and Arlington. Baird garage; few cabins: Dazy and Parkview; all accommodations.) Carthage was settled in 1842 and is the center of one of the richest farming districts in the Ozarks. It has considerable manufacturing activity, including a large powder mill and seven marble quarries, which produce the famous "Carthage Marble"—the only true gray marble in the United States.

On July 5, 1861, the **Battle of Carthage** was fought in the vicinity, between 1,100 Missouri Volunteer Infantry (Union) and 4,000 Missouri State Guardsmen (Confederate) accompanied by 2,000 unarmed recruits. The battle ended in the flight of the Northern forces. Following this battle, there were numerous skirmishes and guerrilla warfare, and Carthage was finally burned by Confederate guerrillas in Sept., 1864. By Jan., 1865, the region was an uninhabited wilderness, to which settlers returned after the war.

In the '70s and '80s, Carthage was the haunt of the notorious woman bandit **BELLE STARR.** Her maiden name was

Myra Belle Shirley, and she spent her girlhood before the Civil War in her father's hotel on the north side of Carthage's court house square. Belle's brother, Bud, a Confederate guerrilla, was killed during the war and the family went to Texas. Belle was an excellent shot and took her brother's place as a member of the band of the guerrilla raider, Quantrill. Her second marriage was to Sam Starr, whose ranch became the headquarters of her band until she was shot by another outlaw.

As you leave Carthage, at **62 mi.** (152 mi.) you pass a large **Municipal Park** (L). From this point until you reach Miami, Okla., about 53 miles, you will find the several communities so closely linked that they are almost indistinguishable as separate towns.

Gas stations at **65 mi.** (149 mi.) and at **67 mi.** (147 mi.).

At **71 mi.** (143 mi.) you are in **CARTERVILLE** (Pop. 1,582; alt. 976'; garage; stores; no cabins or hotel.) This former opulent mining center is now almost a ghost town, with its boarded-up stores, empty buildings, and general air of desolation. Its decline began at the close of World War I when nearby lead and zinc mines were closed. As you leave the town, you pass through gray piles of mine slag or "chat."

73 mi. (141 mi.) **WEBB CITY.** (Pop. 7,033; alt. 1,003';

Midwest hotel; Empire garage; stores.) The fortunes of Webb City were tied up with those of Carterville in the rich lead and zinc mines, but Webb City was able to offset the decay that threatened when the mines declined. It was the site of the first major discovery of lead in the region, when John Webb, a farmer here, uncovered a chunk of pure lead. It is now a small manufacturing center. No major tourist accommodations here.

Just west of Webb City, US 66 (the same alternate US 66 you took at the fork east of Carthage) turns south toward Joplin. US 66 has a city route and a suburban route through Joplin, both meeting in the edge of the business district.

78 mi. (136 mi.) JOPLIN. (Pop. 37,144; alt. 1,009'; radio station WMBH—1450 kc.; hotels: Connor, Keystone, Yates, Virginia; courts: Koronado, Trail Inn, Golden Glow, Castle, Mack's, Gateway, Star, Tivoli Park, Sunset, Joplin Courts, Joy Vista; garages: Rayl-Stanley, Reno Motor Co., Bob Smith's, Bill's; stores; all accommodations. Many courts on U. S. 66 at western approaches to city.)

The Joplin district is one of the greatest producers of zinc ore in the world, and also leads in the production of lead ores. Several large quarries produce 99% pure limestone, from the limestone which underlies all southwest Missouri. Camp Crowder, an Army base in World War II is southeast of here. As you leave Joplin on US 66, you pass **Schifferdecker Park**, which contains an unusually large mineral museum (R).

At the western edge of Joplin, you pass through great piles of "chert" or "chat," the waste from lead and zinc mines. The suburban edge of Joplin is near the **MISSOURI-KANSAS STATE LINE**, at **84 mi.** (130 mi.). One mile beyond is the large smelter of the **EAGLE-PICHER CO.** (R), a great producer of lead and typical of the industry in this famous area.

87 mi. (127 mi.) **GALENA.** (Pop. 4,375; alt. 976′; garages: Phipps and Front St.; small hotel; no cabins; stores; gas; cafes.)

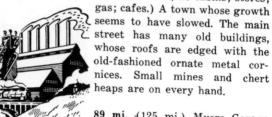

A town whose growth seems to have slowed. The main street has many old buildings, whose roofs are edged with the old-fashioned ornate metal cornices. Small mines and chert heaps are on every hand.

89 mi. (125 mi.) Myers Garage here (L). Shortly afterward you cross **SPRING RIVER**, with a large power plant on its western bank (L). This is the **Empire District Hydro-electric Plant**, furnishing power to over 75 towns. The region here is green and wooded, a welcome change from the drab mines.

90 mi. (124 mi.) **RIVERTON.** (Pop. 104; alt. 900′; Jayhawk Court; gas; limited facilities.)

91 mi. (123 mi.) Gas station at this point.

97 mi. (117 mi.) **BAXTER SPRINGS.** (Pop. 4,921; alt. 842′;

Merry Bales hotel; garages: Pruitt Motor Co. and Tally's; cabin camps include: Baxter, Sunbeam and 66 Camp; small business district with cafes, stores, etc.) A green and quiet town with an ancient, bloody history. In the '60s it was a wide-open cattle town when the railroad ran to here. In 1863, a small Union garrison here was attacked by Confederate guerrilla raiders led by **QUANTRILL,** most noted of the guerrillas. Sites are inadequately marked, and it would be a great improvement if state authorities were to install more markers to this historic locality.

Just west of Baxter Springs, you reach the **KANSAS-OKLAHOMA STATE LINE,** at **98 mi.** (116 mi.). Gas station here; also shops selling mineral specimens. Many lead and zinc mines.

103 mi. (111 mi.) **QUAPAW.** (Pop. 1,054; alt. 840′; Gateway Hotel; Lucy garage; gas; few stores.) Quapaw is located on the old **Quapaw Indian Reservation.** Every July 4th the Indians hold the Quapaw Pow-Wow at "Devil's Promenade," a bluff 6 miles east of here. Elaborate costumes and dances feature the event, to which visitors are welcomed.

The road for the next 100 miles is good: with wide shoulders, generally grassy. The hills are low, the countryside almost flat and with patches of wood.

At **108 mi.** (106 mi.) US 66 turns south. At the curve is a roadside park (R) with tables and fireplaces. Across the railroad (R) is the big plant of the **Eagle-Picher Mining & Smelting Co.,** with large piles of "chat" behind it.

109 mi. (105 mi.) **COMMERCE.** (Pop. 2,422; alt. 805′; only tourist court is O'Brien's Camp on north side of town; Lee Sult's garage; gas; limited facilities.) Commerce is a town composed chiefly of homes of miners, whose cottages and

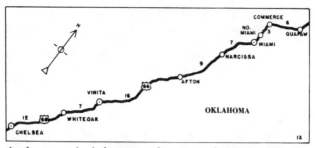

shacks are mingled among the many chat heaps. In the town, where US 66 makes a sharp turn, is a large mineral specimen shop, selling samples of native and other ores for 10c and up.

From here into North Miami, you pass through more chat heaps. at **111 mi.** (103 mi.) is a large **airport** (R) by the side of the road. Air Force fliers were trained here.

112 mi. (102 mi.) **NORTH MIAMI.** (Pop. 393; courts: Butler's, Miami, O'Brien's, and O'Connor's Trailer Park.) Really a suburb of Miami, the community of North Miami has scarcely any business district of its own.

114 mi. (100 mi.) **MIAMI.** (Pop. 8,345; alt. 800′; major hotel: Miami, also Main Hotel; garages: Neosho, B. & M., Norton-Elliott, Miami; tourist court: Sooner State; stores; all facilities.) The town was named after the Miami Indians. **Northeastern A. & M. College** is located here. Prospectors seeking lost Spanish mines around here found rich deposits of zinc and lead instead. As you leave town, you cross the **Neosho River,** and at the edge of town is a small civilian airport and gas stations.

118 mi. (96 mi.) **Roadside park** (R), with several stone tables and fireplaces. At most of these parks, camping is forbidden, the facilities being chiefly for picnicking.

121 mi. (93 mi.) **NARCISSA.** Only one establishment on US 66: a gas station with a grocery and small garage. Nearby is the community: about 25 homes, a school and grain elevator. A similar small community is **AFTON**, at **130 mi.** (84 mi.). (Pop. 1,261; alt. 290'; Baker's Cafe; Northeast garage and Eagle Service Station garage; Acme Court.)

At **135 mi.** (79 mi.) US 66 turns west at Lake Junction gas station (R). On the left is a roadside park with tables. Another gas station at **144 mi.** (70 mi.).

At **146 mi.** (68 mi.) you enter the edge of **VINITA** and pass the **Rodeo Stadium** (L), where the Will Rogers Memorial Rodeo is held each Sept. (Town crowded at that time.) US 66 goes through the main street. (Pop. 5,685; alt. 702'; hotels: Vinita and Cobb; courts: DeLuxe, Ranch Motel, Meek's, 66 Court, Texaco Cabins—all on south side; garages; stores; all facilities.) Vinita was named for a famous sculptress, **Vinita Ream,** who carved the statue of Lincoln now in Washington.

148 mi. (66 mi.) Tip Top Court, with gas and cafe.

149 mi. (65 mi.) **Truck weighing station** (R) of Oklahoma State Highway Dept. A gas station with a small garage is at **150 mi.** (64 mi.)

153 mi. (61 mi.) **WHITEOAK,** a small hamlet with a couple of gas stations and groceries, plus a school and a few homes. No cafes, garages, courts or other accommodations here.

155 mi. (59 mi.) Gas station. At **163 mi.** (51 mi.) is Shadygrove Tourist Camp, with cafe, gas, and garage.

165 mi. (49 mi.) **CHELSEA.** (Pop. 1,642; alt. 723'; courts: Hester and others; garages: Null, Home; cafes: Pig-in-

Pen and Log Cabin; several gas stations; few stores.) A small business district is off US 66 (R). **Will Rogers** used to visit his sister, Mrs. McSpadden, here frequently. Two miles south of here is the site of the first oil well in Oklahoma, completed in 1889.

171 mi. (43 mi.) **BUSHYHEAD.** (Pop. 45; alt. 700'; gas and grocery on US 66; no other facilities.) A village named for a Cherokee Indian chief. An old Indian lookout west of here.

174 mi. (40 mi.) **FOYIL.** (Pop. 170; gas; small garages; groceries; no cafes or courts.) A small hamlet serving the farms and cattle ranches of the region.

179 mi. (35 mi.) **SEQUOYAH.** Listed on the maps as a "town," but actually consisting of a coal loader, a dozen homes, and one gas station and store. Another gas station and grocery at **180 mi.** (34 mi.).

185 mi. (29 mi.) **CLAREMORE.** (Pop. 6,000; alt. 602'; hotels: Mason, Will Rogers, Sequoyah; courts: El Sueno and Cozy Court; Randle´ & Munson garage; all facilities.) Famous as the home of **WILL ROGERS**. A tourist information center on US 66 will direct you to points of interest, chief of which is the $200,000 **Will Rogers Memorial** built in 1938 on a 20-acre plot he owned. The Memorial is less than a mile off US 66 and contains four galleries of dioramas, saddle collections, mementoes, trophies, screen costumes and other remembrances of the cowboy humorist who died in 1935. (Memorial open 8 to 5 daily, free.) Rogers' body was moved here in May, 1944; beside him rests Mrs. Rogers, who died in June, 1944. A heroic bronze statue by Jo Davidson stands in the

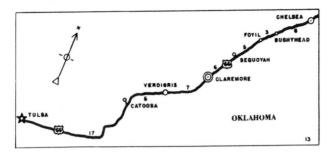

foyer. Memorial services held here each Nov. 4th, Rogers' birthday.

Claremore is also noted for its radium water baths. In the Mason Hotel lobby is a collection of 6,000 guns—the largest individual **gun collection** in the world, assembled by J. M. Davis and including weapons of Emmett Dalton, Pancho Villa, Henry Starr, Cole Younger, Pretty Boy Floyd and others, as well as several ancient pieces.

190 mi. (24 mi.) Gas station and grocery.

192 mi. (22 mi.) **VERDIGRIS.** (Pop. 64; Bowen's garage; gas; groceries; no tourist accommodations or cafe.) Four miles south of here is the site of old Ft. Spunky, used during the Civil War.

195 mi. (19 mi.) Gas and curios at a station just south of a bridge here over the **Verdigris River.**

197 mi. (17 mi.) The hamlet of **CATOOSA** (Pop. 405; alt. 618') lies about one-half mile west of US 66 here.

198 mi. (16 mi.) **LOOKOUT MOUNTAIN** lies off US 66 (R) a short distance. A low, rounded "mountain," it is hardly more than a hill. Formerly an Indian vantage point.

199 mi. (15 mi.) Intersection of US 66 and Oklahoma 33. Gas, garage and cabins here.

200 mi. (14 mi.) US 66 turns sharply west here, and runs straight ahead into Tulsa. At **202 mi.** (12 mi.) is the community of **LYNN LANE**, a suburb of Tulsa, with several gas stations, a small garage and several homes. KVO court here.

Now you enter the outskirts of Tulsa, and proceed toward the center of town. Your speedometer reading ends at a cemetery (R) near the midtown section, at **214 mi.** (0 mi.).

TULSA. (Pop. 142,157; alt. 700'; several hotels including: Adams, Alvin, Bliss, Bradford, Cadillac, Corona, Tulsa, Mayo, Mercer, Oklahoma, Plaza, Seneca and Wells; courts include: Cook's, Park Plaza, Anchor, Baker's, Blue Jay, Campbell's, El Reposo, Mid-Way, Rio, Shady-Rest, Tulsa, Whitt, Will Rogers, Grotto; many courts on both sides of Tulsa; garages: McGee, Apache & Cinn, Hocker; radio stations: KTUL—1170 kc., KOME—1340 kc.; all accommodations.)

Tulsa is Oklahoma's second city, with full tourist facilities. Known as "The Oil Capitol of the World," it is a relatively young city which grew with the oil industry. If you have time, stop at the Chamber of Commerce, 201 Tulsa Bldg., for a map showing an interesting tour of the city. Signs direct you to points of interest such as oil wells, refineries, Spartan aircraft and trailer plants, art center, Indian museums, Tulsa University, prize-winning rose gardens, etc. State fair held here each Sept.; International Petroleum Exposition held here each May of even years.

NOTE: Speedometers differ slightly, so if your mileage readings do not match with those in this Guide Book, make occasional adjustments in your figures as required.

SOME TIPS ON CROSS-COUNTRY DRIVING

Most drivers, accustomed to short trips or city traffic, find long cross-country driving tiring. This is especially true if you are making the trip in the shortest possible time, which requires faster speeds and consequent tenseness on the part of the driver.

The men who drive big trucks know many "tricks of the road," and you will often overhear these devices discussed if you stop for coffee in the roadside cafes truckers frequent.

Don't cut down on your sleep—get plenty. One of the greatest dangers is to fall asleep at the wheel. It's wise to sleep a little longer than you would at home, since you are in a "strange bed" and are more tired physically. Try going to bed early, getting up before dawn, so you can take the road with the first faint light. Roads are more empty in the hours before dawn than in the hours immediately after sunset.

On the road, don't drink too much liquid, because your kidneys will soon proclaim the strain, which is bad enough after several hours' driving anyway. Do not eat heavy meals in the morning or at noon, and avoid starches. It is better to eat lighter and more often, and eat fruit in preference to starchy pastries.

In night driving—if you must drive all night—drive until you feel sleepy, then stop and sleep a while in the car, sitting up. The cramped position will not allow you to sleep long, but the nap will "take the edge off" your sleepiness, and allow you to drive another good stretch before you again feel sleepy.

This section of your trip takes you from Tulsa, Oklahoma, to Oklahoma City. The route is through rolling country-side—once the haunt of Indians, later the territory of

cowmen and "bad men," but now devoted princi-pally to oil and agricul-ture. Part of your route is through a section of

the famous "Cherokee Strip." On week-ends the traffic is somewhat heavier near Oklahoma City. The road is good, but the shoulders are soggy in wet weather. In the smaller towns, brick streets are often bumpy.

As you leave the center of **TULSA** over streets plainly marked with highway signs, you enter upon a wide street. About two miles from the center of town, you pass a shady **PARK** (R) occupying a city block. Set your speed-ometer reading in the margin of the page at this point. **0 mi.** (123 mi.). From this point until you reach Sapulpa, Okla., about 10 miles from here you will scarcely realize you have left Tulsa, since the highway is flanked with a constant succession of business establishments, tourist courts, garages, gas stations, etc.

At **2 mi.** (121 mi.) you pass the **Crystal City Amusement Park** (L). Soon afterwards you enter the suburb of **RED FORK,** an industrial suburb of Tulsa containing many factories. If you are interested in pottery, visit the large **pottery plant** here, which utilizes native clays.

A railroad parallels US 66 on your right from here into Sapulpa.

10 mi. (113 mi.) **SAPULPA.** (Pop. 12,249; St. James hotel;

47

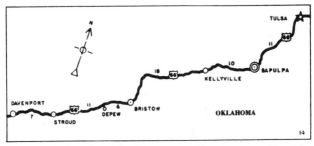

courts: W-E, Elkins, both on east side; garages: Hendrix and Thompson; stores; all accommodations.)

Sapulpa's history goes back to 1886 and is rich in Indian and pioneer lore. It is the center of oil and gas production in the famous **"Glenn Pool"** where fortunes were made in the early oil boom. One pair of investors started with $700 and ran their fortune up to $35 million in 11 years. Now oil is merely a routine business. Sapulpa also has glass factories (you pass the **Liberty Glass Co.** on the east side of town) and also has a large brickyard, which you pass as you leave town going west.

Leaving Sapulpa you pass the **municipal golf course (L)** at **13 mi.** (110 mi.). Soon afterwards, at **16 mi.** (107 mi.) is a roller skating rink and gas station. Just beyond here you begin climbing a one-mile length of winding road, twisting rather sharply upward.

18 mi. (105 mi.) Gas station here, with a few cabins. This part of the route enters a farming territory.

21 mi. (102 mi.) **KELLYVILLE.** (Pop. 647; alt. 764'; cafes; gas; small garage; no tourist accommodations.) A small community with about ten business establishments. At the western edge of town, just before you cross **Little Polecat Creek** is the Devonian Oil Co. Refinery (R).

26 mi. (97 mi.) Gas station here, on the west bank of Polecat Creek. A sign indicates this establishment is the "town" of Heyburn, which is a railroad loading point south of here.

By this time you will have noticed the famous red soil of Oklahoma, which will become a deeper, richer red as you proceed farther west in the state. The road is good, but detours are quite difficult in wet weather if you are routed over a dirt road of this red earth.

30 mi. (93 mi.) Gas station here, with a half-dozen cabins. Other gas stations at **32 mi.** (91 mi.) and at **34 mi.** (89 mi.). Since leaving Tulsa you have seen occasional oil derricks. In the next several miles many more will be seen, although US 66 does not go through main fields.

39 mi. (84 mi.) **BRISTOW.** (Pop. 6,050; alt. 818'; garages: 66 Motor Co. and Bristow Motor Co.; courts: Mac's, Brayton's, Thurman's, Rest-Well, and Bristow Court & Trailer Park; Roland Hotel; stores; all accommodations.) Fifty years ago, Bristow was a Creek Indian trading center. Today it is a major oil and gas center.

At **41 mi.** (82 mi.) is a gas station. At **45 mi.** (78 mi.) US 66 skirts the northern edge of **DEPEW** (Pop. 876), but the only facilities along the highway are gas stations.

51 mi. (72 mi.) At this point you pass over a steel bridge. Just west is what appears to be a good campsite (R), but there is no indication as to whether camping is permitted here or not. There are several such spots along here.

53 mi. (70 mi.) US 66 emerges from a wooded region and passes through a brief stretch of plains along here.

56 mi. (67 mi.) **STROUD.** (Pop. 1,917; alt. 905'; garage: Ford; hotel: Graham; courts: Poplar and two others; gas;

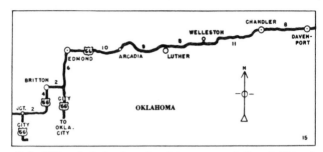

all facilities, but short on tourist accommodations.) Stroud is a busy farm trading center, and US 66 goes down its main street, which is of brick. South of here are deserted government Indian agency buildings, from the days when Sac and Fox tribal affairs were handled there.

63 mi. (60 mi.) **DAVENPORT.** (Pop. 975; alt. 840'; gas; cafes; small garages; small business district; no overnight tourist accommodations.) The many oil derricks which line both sides of US 66 at the eastern edge of town testify to its importance as an Oklahoma oil center.

71 mi. (52 mi.) **CHANDLER.** (Pop. 2,738; alt. 891'; Grace Hotel; LaGere garage; courts: Lincoln, Chandler; all facilities.) In the cemetery here is the grave of Bill Tilghman, a famous frontier marshal in the days of the Territory. Chandler is now an agricultural trading center and ships considerable honey and pecans. In the 1870's every building except a church was leveled by a cyclone.

73 mi. (50 mi.) Here US 66 runs between a dozen oil derricks operated by the Magnolia Petroleum Co. Between the derricks are neat homes. Gas station here. At **78 mi.** (45 mi.) is another gas station with a grocery and garage. More gas at **79 mi.** (44 mi.).

82 mi. (41 mi.) **WELLESTON** is a small community located about one mile north of here. At the crossroads is the Pioneer Tourist Court, with a gas station.

84 mi. (39 mi.) Gas station. **85 mi.** (38 mi.) Dixie Inn cafe and gas station. **87 mi.** (36 mi.) Gas station and Red Cross first aid station. At **89 mi.** (34 mi.) you pass an old cemetery (R) containing a few graves with old-fashioned markers.

90 mi. (33 mi.) **LUTHER.** (Pop. 425; alt. 896'.) The village lies south (L) of US 66. The crossroad lies between two railroad overpasses. Only facility on US 66 is a gas station at the junction. More gas at **94 mi.** (29 mi.).

99 mi. (24 mi.) **ARCADIA.** (Pop. 224; alt. 959'; one cabin court; cafe; gas; grocery and general store.) Once this was a fair-sized little town, but its growth has stopped. A cotton gin indicates one of the chief industries.

As you approach Arcadia from the east, at the edge of town there is a school (R) on top of a hill. Across the road is a **HISTORICAL MARKER** (L) in a field corner, stating: "The Washington Irving Party and a Troop of U. S. Rangers encamped on this spot, October, 1832." Irving, author of "Rip Van Winkle" and other tales, traveled in this region and wrote his "Tour of the Prairies." He is said to have shot a buffalo on the banks of Coffee Creek south of here.

101 mi. (22 mi.) Gas station. More gas at **102 mi.** (21 mi.). Next 5 miles is brick pavement with many short hills.

104 mi. (19 mi.) Gas and grocery. **105 mi.** (18 mi.) gas. At **107 mi.** (16 mi.) brick pavement and sharp hills end.

109 mi. (14 mi.) **EDMOND.** (Pop. 4,202; alt. 1191'; Martin's court; Royce cafe is good; Chet Moore garage;

stores.) This busy community has a flour mill and other small industries. The **Central State Teachers College** is here, established in 1891. US 66 makes a sharp turn (L) in the center of Edmond and runs straight ahead into the business district of Oklahoma City, about 12 miles south.

112 mi. (11 mi.) **Memorial Cemetery** (L), most beautiful in Oklahoma, with its 135 landscaped acres and 72-foot tower containing chimes. **Wiley Post**, famous aviator killed in a crash when flying with Will Rogers, is buried here.

If you do not care to stop in Oklahoma City, it is possible to turn right on "Belt Line 66" and cut across the northern suburbs of the city and save considerable time. This Guide Book is written for the through traveler taking this cut-off. At **114 mi.** (9 mi.) you pass the transmitter tower of radio station KOMA (L) and one mile south of here US 66 (Belt Line) turns sharply right. Two gas stations here. If taking the cut-off, turn right; if going into Oklahoma City, go straight ahead. For data on Oklahoma City, see description on next page.

On Belt Line 66, you pass the transmitter towers of radio station WKY and enter **BRITTON** at **117 mi.** (6 mi.). (Pop. 2,239; alt. 1,213'; Ford garage; Owl court; stores and cafes.) After passing through Britton's three blocks of stores, Belt Line 66 turns sharply south (L) and enters the northern suburbs of Oklahoma City. At **118 mi.** (5 mi.) you pass Nichol's Hills (R), a major home sub-division.

At **121 mi.** (2 mi.) Belt Line 66 turns sharply (R) and crosses the street car tracks. Watch for this turn. Now you continue west two miles through a residential district until you reach the intersection of City 66 and Belt Line 66 at **123 mi.** (0 mi.) A convenient marker for this intersection is the Stewart Lumber Co. yard here. This ends your speedometer reading for this section of the trip. West from this intersection are many fine tourist courts along US 66.

If you have decided to visit Oklahoma City, you will find many points of interest worth seeing.

OKLAHOMA CITY. (Pop. 204,424; alt. 1,196'; radio stations: KOCY—1340 kc., KOMA—1520 kc., KTOK—1400 kc., and WKY—930 kc.; several hotels, major ones including Black, Kingkade, Park-O-Tell, Oklahoma Biltmore, and Skirvin; plenty of garages and all other facilities. (Good cafe is Dolores Restaurant.) The Oklahoma State Fair is held here late each September; Flower Show in early October; Livestock Show in late March.

Oklahoma City is the largest city in the state, and contains the state capitol and Oklahoma City University. The big oil field here began 18 years ago, and there are nearly 1,000 oil derricks in the southwest part of town. Oil derricks are located within sight of the capitol building. The tallest building is the 32-story bank structure which can be seen from all approaches to the city. In the State Historical Society Building is a museum of old coaches, wagons, autos, with Indian relics and other objects. This city really "grew overnight" in 1889 when it was opened for settlement. By sunset of April 22 in that year, over 10,000 people camped when the famous Cherokee Strip was opened, and within 24 hours the open prairie became a great community here.

For directions to local points of interest in any major city, visit the local Chamber of Commerce which usually has folders and maps available free.

BOOKS ABOUT HIGHWAY 66 LOCALITIES

US Highway 66 runs through territory made famous as the locale of many stories and books. Reading these tales will greatly increase your enjoyment of the trip. They may be read before or after the trip, and also form the ideal reading for passengers who like to read occasionally en route. Following are a few of the more famous books which might be recommended:

THE GRAPES OF WRATH, by John Steinbeck. (Available in a 25c edition.) The story of an Oklahoma farm family who lost their farm during the Dust Bowl days of the 30's and journeyed by car over US 66 to California. Their route over US 66 was approximately from Oklahoma City to Barstow, Calif., from whence they turned northwest. Many fine descriptions of scenes along US 66.

THE SAGA OF BILLY THE KID, by Walter Noble Burns. (Also available in a 25c edition.) The fictionalized biography of the West's most famous desperado, who had killed a man for each year of his life when he was himself killed at the age of 21. Born William Bonney in New York City, he roamed east central New Mexico, southeast of Santa Rosa, until killed in 1880. The book tells much of life in this region in the 70's.

LAUGHING BOY, by Oliver LaFarge. (Also available at 25c.) A superb story of native Navajo life in the country through which US 66 passes from Gallup to Flagstaff.

THE SHEPHERD OF THE HILLS, by Harold Bell Wright. A best-selling book about life in the Ozark country south of Springfield, Missouri. The locale is similar to the Ozarks through which US 66 passes. The author was a pastor in Lebanon, Mo., for a while.

CHAPTER VI
OKLAHOMA CITY TO AMARILLO, TEXAS

This section of your trip over US Highway 66 takes you from Oklahoma City to Amarillo, Texas. Shortly after you cross the Oklahoma-Texas State Line, the "Real West" will

open before you as if a theatre curtain were suddenly lifted. The states of Illinois, Missouri, Kansas and Oklahoma each have their attractions of hills, streams, and pioneer history, but their general aspect is nevertheless quite similar. To the average person, the "west" means barren plains, high mountains, Mexicans and pueblo Indians. The plains, at least, begin in Texas, and the other attractions soon follow.

Whether you have "by-passed" Oklahoma City or have been in the city itself, both city and bypass routes rejoin at the northwest corner of the city.

0 mi. (273 mi.) Junction of City 66 and Belt Line 66. The Stewart Lumber Co. yard at this corner is your landmark. Mark your speedometer reading in the margin of this page.

In the next two miles you will pass several good tourist courts along US 66, including: Boyer, Deluxe, Rush, Carlyle, Major, Oklahoma, and Hutchison.

4 mi. (269 mi.) **BETHANY.** (Pop. 2,590; alt. 1,212′; garages; stores; cafe; no courts.) This town was founded in 1906 by members of the Nazarene Church, who established a college here and laid down certain community regulations which still stand. No cigarettes, tobacco or alcoholic drinks are sold in the town, and there are no theatres.

6 mi. (267 mi.) Cross a steel bridge over the **North Canadian River.** For the next two miles you will pass **LAKE OVERHOLSER,** a beautiful lake which furnishes the water supply of Oklahoma City. Lakeview Court is the major tourist court along the road here. At the lake edge are speedboats which will take you on a fast lake ride for a small sum. Many tourists pull over to the side of the road here for a short rest in the shade, while they watch the water. The lake was built thirty years ago by a river dam.

11 mi. (262 mi.) **YUKON.** (Pop. 1,660; alt. 1,295'; garages: Barrett, Ford, Dependable; courts: Star, Yukon, Valley; stores; cafes.) As you enter Yukon from the east, you pass the Dobry Flour Mills and other mills. The soil around here is very rich, and grain crops are popular.

12 mi. (261 mi.) Gas. **14 mi.** (259 mi.) Gas. **17 mi.** (256 mi.) Gas. A few miles farther, you will strike a stretch of widened highway running into El Reno.

23 mi. (250 mi.) **EL RENO.** (Pop. 10,078; alt. 1,358'; hotels Kerfoot, Southern; courts: Eagle, Colonial Court, Phillips; garages: El Reno and Rother; stores; all facilities.) The town gets its name from the nearby fort, which you will pass west of town. US 66 traverses brick streets through the town at present. The town was originally larger, during the opening of Indian lands to settlement.

28 mi. (245 mi.) Entrance (L) to **U. S. Southwestern Reformatory.** Costing over a million dollars, this prison was built to house violators of Federal laws, especially first offenders or "short-termers." (No admittance to visitors.)

30 mi. (243 mi.) Entrance to **FORT RENO** (R), an Army post established prior to 1876 to protect a nearby Indian agency. For many decades it was a great "remount" station, supplying army horses, and horses can still be seen on

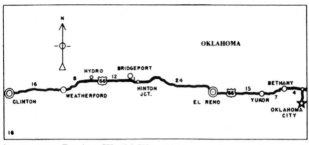

its ranges. During World War II it was also a prisoner of war camp. The fort stretches along US 66 for nearly four miles.

35 mi. (238 mi.) Gas stations here. US 66 now travels through what is known as "short grass" range country—the first indication of the vast Texas plains to come.

38 mi. (235 mi.) Gas. **41 mi.** (232 mi.) Gas. Gas also at **42 mi.** (231 mi.). Small groceries at these gas stations.

You are now nearing the point where US 66 crosses the South Canadian River, and as the highway winds around and over the river banks, you will find some noticeable grades. At **44 mi.** (229 mi.) you drop down a grade (gas station at top of next hill) and climb to the top of a grade which then drops 150 ft. in a mile, bringing you to a bridge across the **SOUTH CANADIAN RIVER.** At the eastern end of the bridge is a cafe and gas station. The cement bridge is ¾ of a mile long, most of it over shallow flats dry during most of the year. On the west bank you make a climb up onto the plains again.

50 mi. (223 mi.) **HINTON JUNCTION.** A state road runs 8 miles south to Hinton at this point. Rodeo in Hinton each August. At the junction is a large roadside park with several tables, fireplaces, and water. Nearby are a cafe, gas station, garage, and two small courts. Just west on US 66 is Leon Little's cafe with gas and a few cabins.

51 mi. (222 mi.) **BRIDGEPORT.** (Pop. 302; alt. 1,424'.) A small town about one mile off US 66 (R). At the junction of the Bridgeport road with US 66 are several gas stations and three tourist courts: Yount's, Guy's, and Harvey House.

59 mi. (214 mi.) A stone picnic table here, under the trees (L), with a gas station nearby.

60 mi. (213 mi.) Gas station. Two more stations ahead, about a mile apart.

63 mi. (210 mi.) Road right to **HYDRO**, about a mile off US 66. (Pop. 759; alt. 1,475'; Kirk's Court.)

64 mi. (209 mi.) Two small tourist courts here. Gas station at **65 mi.** (208 mi.). Just west of an underpass at **67 mi.** (206 mi.) is another stone picnic table under a tree (R).

71 mi. (202 mi.) **WEATHERFORD.** (Pop. 2,504; alt. 1,645'; 66 court; garages: Crossley, Friesen's, and Ford; Means Hotel; stores.) A teachers' college is located here. Weatherford is an agricultural trading center. Hume Motel is on US 66 one mile east of Weatherford.

75 mi. (198 mi.) Small tourist camp. Gas at **81 mi.** (192 mi.) and at **83 mi.** (190 mi.).

87 mi. (186 mi.) **CLINTON.** (Pop. 6,726; alt. 1,564'; Hotel Calmez is good, so is Harry's cafe; Jones garage; stores; cafes; courts are on west approach to town: Neptune and Petty's.) Clinton arose slowly at the turn of the century and is a trading and shipping center for the surrounding farms. An Indian tubercular hospital is located here. At west edge of town is a large roadside park (L).

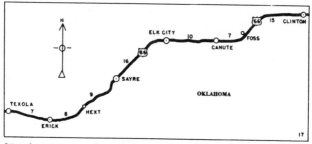

95 mi. (178 mi.) Gas. Shortly west of here US 66 goes up over some low hills of rich red earth prominent in this region. Another gas station at **100 mi.** (173 mi.).

102 mi. (171 mi.) Road right here one-half mile to FOSS. (Pop. 306; alt. 1,622'; garage.) Gas station and cafe at junction. During World War II, there was a Naval Base south of here.

105 mi. (168 mi.) Cafe at this point; no gas. One mile west of here, US 66 skirts a lake, created by a dam. At **107 mi.** (166 mi.) is a gas station with garage and a few cabins.

109 mi. (164 mi.) CANUTE. (Pop. 374; alt. 1,910'; gas; Mahl Bros. garage; 1 trailer court but no cabins.) At the eastern edge of town is a Catholic cemetery with some unusual bronze statuary. The town itself contains several cotton gins in sheet metal structures: the Planters Ginning Co. and Canute Gin, among others.

110 mi. (163 mi.) Stone picnic table under trees (L). The red soil in this area is the deepest red to be found in Oklahoma, and the farms are reputedly prosperous.

119 mi. (154 mi.) ELK CITY. (Pop. 5,021; alt. 1,912'; radio station KASA—1240 kc.; hotels: Casa Grande and Story; courts: Bungalo, Elk, Royal, Motor Inn, Star — on west edge of town; good cafe is Campbell's; hospital in town; garages: Brewer's and Galloway's; stores.) Elk City, with its shady streets, brisk business section and quiet homes, offers a distinct mid-western appearance and might be a town in Indiana or Ohio. It is in this community that an unusual experiment in group medical care is being conducted: each family pays $25 a year, for which they receive all medical attention. The Farmers Union has supported the project, which was launched by a local physician. The town has one main business street, which is crossed by US 66. Rodeo stadium at west edge of town.

121 mi. (152 mi.) Gas. **122 mi.** (151 mi.) Stone table under trees (R). **126 mi.** (147 mi.) One establishment here offers gas, grocery, light auto repairs, and a few cabins.

127 mi. (146 mi.) Another stone picnic table (R). More gas at **129 mi.** (144 mi.).

135 mi. (138 mi.) SAYRE. (Pop. 3,037; alt. 1,810′; Draper garage; courts: Chief, Kastle Kottages, and Red, White and Blue; few small hotels, cafes; plenty of facilities.) US 66 enters this quiet town, drops down a slight hill and turns right in the business district whose one main street ends at the courthouse. Joseph Benton, who took the stage name of **Giuseppe Bentonelli** when he became a Metropolitan Opera star in 1935, came here as a child and still has relatives here. **Jess Willard**, famous prize fighter, once drove a wagon freight line from here and also ran a lodging house.

As you leave Sayre you cross a concrete bridge a half-mile long over the north fork of the **Red River**, and later pass the city park (L) with its playground, stone tables, and fireplaces, at **137 mi.** (136 mi.).

140 mi. (133 mi.) A dirt road runs off (R) here to the

Oklahoma Salt Works, whose stacks can be seen from US 66. This works produces coarse salt, and in early days cattle were driven to salt springs such as these, in order to give the animals their needed supply of precious salt.

144 mi. (129 mi.) **HEXT.** Not a community—just a gas station, and an indication that from here on west many of the "towns" shown on usual road maps often contain no more than one building. Population figures do not necessarily reflect the true "population" of the "town" itself, but list those in the surrounding area to whom the point is a mail address or registration point. The countryside along here is full of brush and is not fully inhabited.

148 mi. (125 mi.) Gas station and grocery.

152 mi. (121 mi.) **ERICK.** (Pop. 1,591; alt. 2,055'; Elms garage; cafes; gas; DeLuxe Court, also Erick Ct. and Trailer Park; stores.) US 66 crosses the one main street of the town, which is the first town you encounter, going west, which has any of the true "western" look, with its wide, sun-baked street, frequent horsemen, occasional sidewalk awnings, and similar touches.

156 mi. (117 mi.) Gas station. As you near the Texas line, the trees thin out into low scrub and brush.

159 mi. (114 mi.) **TEXOLA.** (Pop. 337; alt. 2,148'; gas; cafes; no courts; limited facilities.) This sun-baked small town has an old section of stores which truly savor of pioneer days. Notice them to your right on the town's one main cross street. They have sidewalk awnings of wood and metal, supported by posts. Old timers still lounge on the corners.

160 mi. (113 mi.) Cross **TEXAS-OKLAHOMA STATE LINE.** At once the road improves, and a decorative stone

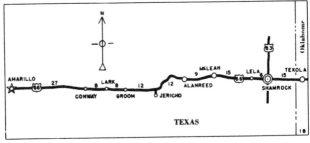

marker welcomes you to this vast state. US 66 crosses a square, projecting northern section of the state, known as the "Panhandle," taking this name probably from the thin "handle" of Oklahoma which projects across, just above the northern line of this region. Texas has wide, splendid roads, with excellent shoulders. There are many roadside parks throughout this part of the state. You have been climbing steadily and slowly since you left Oklahoma City, but the rise has been hardly noticeable.

162 mi. (111 mi.) Roadside park here (L), with stone table under trees. A pleasant place for a casual lunch.

167 mi. (106 mi.) Gas station here. In this section, homes are supplied with natural gas from the surrounding rich fields. Meters are noticeable at the roadside by each home. Many homes have "windmill" generators, too.

168 mi. (105 mi.) US 66 here runs between several oil derricks, operated by the Phillips Petroleum Co. and the Magnolia Petroleum Co.

174 mi. (99 mi.) **SHAMROCK.** (Pop. 3,123; alt. 2,310'; Johnson Hotel; courts: Cross Road, Victoria, North End, 20 Trees, and Shamrock; garages: Burcham and Buck's; plenty of cafes—Dixie is good; all facilities.) Shamrock is obviously an oil town, and one of the most important oil centers in the rich Panhandle field. Many plants here produce carbon black, others are gasoline extraction plants. There are many large facilities producing natural gas—a former waste by-product. The main business section of Shamrock is off US 66.

180 mi. (93 mi.) **LELA.** A small settlement, consisting of five gas stations, a cafe and a post office. No tourist accommodations.

For the next several miles, "windbreaks" can be seen along the highway—sometimes on the left, sometimes on the right, occasionally on both sides. The government has planted these "staggered" rows of trees to break the winds which drive down from the north, and thus prevent snowdrifts in winter and dust storms and erosion in the summer. These plantings are part of a huge project which spreads over thousands of square miles.

190 mi. (83 mi.) Two gas stations, one with cafe.

192 mi. (81 mi.) A gas station with grocery and cafe and a small garage—all in one establishment.

195 mi. (78 mi.) **McLean.** (Pop. 1,489; alt. 2,812'; Chevrolet garage; Hindman Hotel; courts: 20 Trees, H&H, Last Chance Court; gas; cafes; stores.) During World War II, a large prisoner of war camp was located just east of here.

Leaving McLean, you begin to enter on the vast Texas plains. In places, the plains are broken by deep "washes" or gullies, caused by erosion during rains. You will encounter several of these in the next 20 miles. The first sizable one is at **203 mi.** (70 mi.), where the road dips into a wash about 75 feet deep and climbs the opposite side.

204 mi. (69 mi.) **ALANREED.** (Pop. 1,489; alt. 2,993';

Ranch House court; gas; cafes; few stores.) Some of the homes in this small town appear old enough to have survived from pioneer days.

212 mi. (61 mi.) Two of the deeper washes occur at this point. Short, steep grades down and up. US 66 now winds in great sweeping curves, down and up through several deep washes which present short grades. Gas station at **216 mi.** (57 mi.) at junction of road (L) to **Jericho.**

Now you are upon the vast **High Plains** of the eastern Texas Panhandle. Straight, paved highways and great, efficient ranches now obliterate all traces of the big herds of buffalo which once roamed here, together with Indians: the Kiowas and Comanches. Mexican shepherds coming up from the south established the first small villages here,

 living with little friction among the Indians. With the coming of the cattlemen, the Mexicans departed but the Indians resisted, often desperately. Beneath the land lie deposits of helium and oil; the rich soil still provides cattle pasture but there are huge farms growing wheat and other grains.

The weather here is very fickle: storms of snow or rain come up suddenly on days which begin with sunshine; the unbelievably fierce winds, or "northers," bring sudden temperature drops and sometimes whip up clouds of sand. Trees are so scarce and other landmarks so infrequent that early settlers often marked their trails with stakes. The newcomer to this region is impressed with the almost limitless emptiness of the countryside.

228 mi. (45 mi.) **GROOM.** (Pop. 475; alt. 3,214′; small

hotel, Wall's cafe and several others; gas; garages; stores.)
A farming community, whose implement stores and grain
elevators serve the countryside.

Continuing on the treeless, flat plain, US 66 lies straight
as a dropped arrow. At **LARK, 236 mi.** (37 mi.) are more
grain elevators, a gas station with a store and postoffice,
and a few railroad houses.

From this point west to the Arizona-California State Line,
be on the alert for cattle crossing the highway, especially
between dusk and dawn. Fences often break, and the animals amble slowly along and across the highways.

244 mi. (29 mi.) **CONWAY.** (Gas; small garage; cafe;
store; one small court; limited facilities.) No gas station
for the next 25 miles! Along Texas highways, dry uprooted
tumbleweeds often roll across the road.

263 mi. (10 mi.) Entrance (R) to **Amarillo Army Air Field,**
where giant bombers and smaller pursuit craft trained
during World War II.

Shortly afterwards, you begin to enter the outskirts of
Amarillo and reach the center of town at **273 mi.** (0 mi.).
As you enter Amarillo, you will notice several huge grain
elevators (L) along US 66.

AMARILLO. (Pop. 70,000; alt. 3,676'; radio stations:
KFDA—1230 kc., and KGNC—1440 kc.; 4 leading hotels
and 40 smaller ones; 36 auto courts; many garages; all
facilities.)

This early cow-town has become a bustling center of Panhandle activity: it is a wholesale center, oil headquarters, cattle shipping point, and railroad center. Amarillo is an outstanding retail market for all types of leather goods. Events include a Stock Show in March and the Tri-State Fair each September. Amarillo is a growing air terminal. Old-timers state that in its early days, Amarillo had many homes built of stretched buffalo hides.

Hotels: Amarillo, Capitol, Herring, Pioneer, Ross, Milner, Blackstone, Elk; courts: Grande, Longhorn Log Lodges, Pueblo, Smith's, Spanish, Tha Best, Royal Palace, Graycourt, Ama-Tone, True-Rest, Pueblo, Forest Hill and Casa Mia. Garages include: Amarillo Auto Clinic, Amarillo Safety Lane, Electric Motor Service.

The post office in Amarillo is the location-point ending this section of your trip. US 66 goes through the center of town, and most of the courts are on the east side.

Twenty-five miles southwest of Amarillo is **Palo Duro Canyon,** worth visiting if you are spending any time in the vicinity of Amarillo. The Canyon is a chasm hundreds of feet deep and several miles long. If you want to ride a real Texas cow pony, you can hire one at the entrance to the park here.

One of the features of the southwest, pleasantly new to the easterner, are the cool nights, which are first noticed around Amarillo and which are found throughout the southwest, including California. As soon as the sun goes down, the temperature begins to drop, and even on warm days, a blanket will be welcome at night. If you are driving west during the summer, a coat is often welcome for night driving.

CHAPTER VII
AMARILLO, TEXAS, TO ALBUQUERQUE, NEW MEXICO

Now you enter the true west, on this leg of your journey over US 66 from Amarillo, Texas, to Albuquerque. New

Mexico. Your trip takes you over the old "Staked Plains," past legendary mountains, up to an altitude over 7,000 feet, through Indian country and cattle ranges, past the haunts of Billy the Kid and other outlaws, into the city of the Con-

quistadores: Albuquerque, New Mexico's metropolis.

0 mi. (304 mi.) Leave Amarillo mid-town (post office). Note your speedometer reading in the margin of the page at this point. If starting your trip here. be sure to read Chapter I.

3 mi. (301 mi.) Pass a Veterans Hospital (R). US 66 makes a well-banked curve to the right, and at **7 mi.** (297 mi.) you pass the **UNITED STATES HELIUM PLANT** (L). The plant is operated by the U. S. Dept. of the Interior, and produces nearly half the world's supply of helium. During World War II it was heavily guarded. A gas station is nearby.

13 mi. (291 mi.) **BUSHLAND.** (Pop. 21; gas; store; no tourist facilities.) A few railroad buildings, three grain elevators and a church complete this small village on the flat Texas plains.

22 mi. (282 mi.) **WILDORADO.** (Pop. 101; Wildorado garage; gas; cafe; grocery; no tourist accommodations.) Like

Bushland, this small hamlet has only a few homes and the ever-present grain elevators to serve surrounding farms.

Now you are upon the "STAKED PLAINS," or "Llano Estacado" as the Spaniards called it. The origin of the name is disputed, but is generally taken to be derived from the legend that early pioneers drove stakes along their trails for lack of natural landmarks to guide them. Great Indian battles occurred on these plains, and they were the haunt of myriad buffalo. Adventuring Spaniards found them a dangerous desolation and many venturesome pioneers died here from thirst and Indian arrows. Later the plains were utilized by the cattle barons, and today most of the Texas section is devoted to grain production.

36 mi. (268 mi.) **VEGA.** (Pop. 515; alt. 4,030'; gas; cafes; three small auto courts; light auto repairs.) Vega derives its livelihood from tourists. and from shipments of grain and cattle. North of here about 22 miles is the ghost town of **TASCOSA.** Seventy years ago a store was located here, and the place soon boomed into a sizeable cowtown to which the cowboys went to "let off steam." It developed a rough reputation and its "boot hill" cemetery grew. Familiar characters were Bat Masterson, Billy the Kid, and others famous on both sides of the law. Today it is the location of **BOYS RANCH,** a project similar to the famous "Boys' Town."

45 mi. (259 mi.) **LANDERGIN.** Listed on many maps as a "town," but actually consisting of a few railroad homes across the railroad tracks, but offering no tourist facilities—not even gas.

51 mi. (253 mi.) **ADRIAN.** (Pop. 250; cafe; gas; no garage or other tourist facilities.) Here, also, the village consists of a few homes, grain elevators, and the usual gas sta-

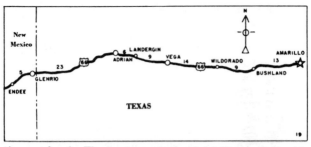

tions and cafe. The next gas station is at **56 mi.** (248 mi.). At **61 mi.** (243 mi.) is a state maintained roadside park with tables and fireplaces. No water.

74 mi. (230 mi.) **GLENRIO.** (Pop. 84; store; gas; no tourist facilities.) This town is shown on maps of both Texas and New Mexico, possibly justified by the fact that the **TEXAS-NEW MEXICO STATE LINE** is located here, with the railroad station east of the line, but with all the business establishments west of the line.

Now you are in New Mexico, a state rich with history. For the most part, US 66 through New Mexico is not as wide or well-paved as in Texas. Until recently, it has been deeply pitted in many places, but the state is conducting an extensive program of highway improvement and is giving special attention to US 66. Since the region is often very arid, it is wise to carry a spare container of water now for your car, and drinking water would come in handy, too. Don't turn off on any side roads without inquiring locally as to road conditions, etc.

79 mi. (225 mi.) **ENDEE.** (Pop. 110; gas; small garage; grocery and a scant handful of cabins.) Only three establishments in this hamlet including its school.

88 mi. (216 mi.) **BARD.** (Pop. 26; alt. 4,290′; gas and garage.) This "town" consists of a single building, but it includes a post office.

94 mi. (210 mi.) **SAN JON.** (Pop. 250; alt. 4,192′; **gas**; garages: San Jon garage and San Jon Implement Co.; two courts; cafes; small hotel; stores.) San Jon is still a center where cowboys can come for Saturday night relaxation, and has performed this function for over two generations. **State truck inspection station** here.

The "J" in San Jon is sounded as a Spanish "J"—like an "h"—San "Hone." The same applies to other place names on US 66: Tijeras, Navajo, Mojave, Cajon, all given the "h" sound. The "i" in Spanish words is sounded "ee."

102 mi. (202 mi.) Gas station. At **110 mi.** (194 mi.) is a **HISTORICAL MARKER: COMANCHE TRAIL.** Text reads: "Through this area passed the Comanche Trails, originally used by the Comanche Indians to follow buffalo herds. Later they were employed as early trade routes. Pedro Vial returned over a Comanche Trail from his initial trip between Santa Fe and St. Louis about 1790. Bootleg traders utilized the routes by 1850."

Another gas station at **112 mi.** (192 mi.). At this point you will notice a squat flat-topped mountain ahead: off to the left. This is **TUCUMCARI MOUNTAIN,** whose legend is explained by the **HISTORICAL MARKER** at **115 mi.** (189 mi.). Text reads: "Tucumcari Mt. Elevation 4,967 ft. 4 miles off road. An Indian legend recalled by the late Chief Geronimo tells that the mountain obtained its name from two young lovers, Tocom and Kari, who died a tragic death. Tocom was slain in a duel with a rival lover, and Kari took her own life."

120 mi. (184 mi.) **TUCUMCARI.** (Pop. 6,194; alt. 4,100′; radio station KTNM—1400 kc.; garages: Waller Motor Co.,

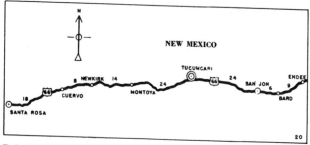

Pelzer and Tucumcari Motor Co.; hotels: Randle, Elk, Vorenberg, and Davis; courts include: Lin's, Travelers, LaNora, Star, White Cottage, Grande, Blue Swallow, Tocom-Kari, Comanche and Venetian; stores; cafes; all accommodations.)

Before the railroad, Tucumcari was a small village where early cowmen came for supplies. A recent vast irrigation project has brought steady growth in the population of the region, which now raises considerable grain. The Sheriff's Posse Rodeo is held here each year—usually in mid-August. Tucumcari is quite a tourist center.

The **time zone changes** here from Central Time to Mountain Time. Westbound tourists should set their watches back one hour; going east, advance watches an hour.

Leaving Tucumcari, your next real cafe and major garage is 62 miles ahead, at **Santa Rosa.** You are still on the plains of the **LLANO ESTACADO,** but shortly west of Tucumcari you begin to climb up off the plains. At **125 mi.** (179 mi.) you pass the entrance to **Tucumcari State Park** (L). A marker at this point, recently defaced, states this was a point on Coronado's route in 1541.

127 mi. (177 mi.) The highway at this point climbs to the top of the **BLUFFS OF THE LLANO ESTACADO.** Mark-

71

ing the western edge of this mighty plain, the steep bluffs and rock formations formed convenient rendezvous spots for cattle rustlers and renegades who plundered the vast herds of early cattle kings in this region until the six-guns of the cowmen and the carbines of U. S. cavalry brought law and order to the district.

The road continues winding through ranch country, with several short hills. Often at a turn of the road or at the top of a rise, a dramatic view of the countryside is revealed. **141 mi.** (163 mi.) Here US 66 passes an **OLD CEMETERY** (L), originally a "boot hill" in the roaring days of nearby Montoya, but now a burial ground for the Mexican people of the vicinity, who decorate the graves with bits of colored china, glass, broken toys and other bric-a-brac.

MONTOYA, just beyond the cemetery, was once a busy town, but it is now merely a loading point for the railroad. (Pop. 125; alt. 4,326'; 2 gas stations; 1 store; no cafe, courts, or garage.) Across the railroad tracks (R) stands an ancient hotel and the ruins of a once-busy little town.

West of Montoya the road winds and climbs through country which becomes more rugged, with rock ledges, mesquite, and stunted trees. Tourists with trailers often camp along here. This part of New Mexico was traversed by early cattle herds and was the haunt of **Billy the Kid.**

149 mi. (155 mi.) **HISTORICAL MARKER: GOODNIGHT TRAIL.** Text reads: "Cowboys who followed bawling herds of cattle from the grasslands of Texas and New Mexico to markets in Colorado, Wyoming, and Kansas, carved a picturesque niche in the history of New Mexico. The Old Goodnight Cattle Trail, blazed in 1866, is crossed by Highway 66 near here."

154 mi. (150 mi.) Gas station.

156 mi. (148 mi.) **NEWKIRK.** (Pop. 115; alt. 4,330'; 4 gas stations, 2 lunchrooms, few cabins; De Baca's Trading Post; no garage or other facilities.) Newkirk's main importance today is its location at the junction of a road (R) to the large **CONCHAS DAM,** 25 miles distant.

Leaving Newkirk, you will notice sections of earth which are a rich terra-cotta in color.

164 mi. (140 mi.) **CUERVO.** (Pop. 128; alt. 4,840'; few gas stations; groceries; no cafe, garage, or other tourist accommodations.) A scant dozen

dwellings comprise this small town. "Cuervo" is Spanish for "small raven." The highway continues to climb and wind over the mesas. From here into Santa Rosa, about 18 miles distant, there will be a few long grades, none of them very difficult.

178 mi. (126 mi.) **HISTORICAL MARKER: TRAIL OF 49'ERS.** Text reads: "Gold seekers in their mad rush to California followed several trails. In 1849, Capt. Marcy and Lt. Simpson conducted a party of gold seekers from Fort Smith, Arkansas. Their route, which parallels Highway 66 to Albuquerque, followed an earlier trail blazed in 1840 by Josiah Gregg."

At **179 mi.** (125 mi.) the highway drops 150 feet in one mile.

181 mi. (123 mi.) Gas station.

182 mi. (122 mi.) **SANTA ROSA.** (Pop. 2,310; alt. 4,600'; garages: Central Motor Co. and Sterling; courts: Santa

Rosa, Yucca, and about 10 others; Sahuaro Trading Post; Jack's Cafe is good; Midland Hotel; stores; all facilities.) Most of Santa Rosa's population is of Spanish descent, and the town began with an early large rancho. It is a county seat.

If your car needs attention, better check it at Santa Rosa, because the next major community is Albuquerque, about 122 miles west.

As you leave Santa Rosa, you cross the famous **PECOS RIVER** at the west edge of town. **HISTORICAL MARKER: CORONADO'S ROUTE** on west bank of river. Text reads: "The journey of Francisco Vasquez Coronado, first explorer of New Mexico, to the mythical province of Quivira, lying to the northeast, was halted near here for four days in the spring of 1541, while the army built a bridge of logs across the Pecos River."

West of Santa Rosa, you begin climbing the range which lies between here and Albuquerque. Just west of Santa Rosa are several fairly steep grades, then you have stretches of gentle grades, followed by steeper climbs.

Four miles west of Santa Rosa you pass a gas station at **185 mi.** (119 mi.) and then climb 200 ft. in one mile. You continue climbing more grades, and at **191 mi.** (113 mi.) you are up over one mile high (5.280 ft.).

At **201 mi.** (103 mi.) is a junction with US 84 (R). Two gas stations at this corner. In the next eight miles you continue climbing, rising another 400 feet. At **211 mi.** (93 mi.) is one establishment: **gas, cafe, garage**—including tow car service for cars which cannot make the grades.

214 mi. (90 mi.) Two establishments here: gas, cafe, two cabins, light auto repairs.

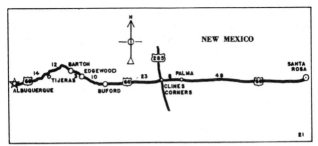

US 66 continues climbing. Gas station at **215 mi.** (89 mi.). About 6,000 feet above sea level at this point. More gas at **219 mi.** (85 mi.), also at **221 mi.** (83 mi.) and again at **224 mi.** (80 mi.).

Along this stretch of US 66 you begin to leave the bare plains and enter a region of short scrub, mostly pinon and juniper. You continue climbing steadily until you reach **PALMA**, at **233 mi.** (71 mi.) This "town," which is listed as having a "population" of 20, consists of only one building: a gas station.

Just west of Palma, you begin one of the steepest climbs yet encountered on your trip west: up 200 feet in one mile. At the top is a short stretch which climbs slowly, with a gas station and cafe here, at **235 mi.** (69 mi.). In the next two miles you continue climbing another 200 feet.

(NOTE: This Guide Book is written for the westbound traveler, hence to the eastbound traveler all "grades up" will be downgrades, and vice versa.)

Soon the climb eases off. At **238 mi.** (66 mi.) is a gas station. Shortly west of here, you can see a high peak in the distance (L). This is **CERRO PEDERNAL.**

At **241 mi.** (63 mi.) you reach **CLINE'S CORNERS.** One

building here, housing a gas station and cafe. West of here, you continue to climb slowly, on a stretch almost level. At **243 mi.** (61 mi.) the road begins to drop. You are up almost 7,000 feet along here.

Now you are on a 20-mile downgrade. In the next three miles you drop about 250 feet, until you reach a gas station at **246 mi.** (58 mi.). Then you descend another 350 feet in the next five miles, to another gas station with a few cabins, at **251 mi.** (53 mi.).

Still dropping, you reach a **HISTORICAL MARKER: GREGG'S TRAIL**, at **252 mi.** (52 mi.). The text reads: "Josiah Gregg, frontiersman and trail blazer, established a trade route between Fort Smith, Arkansas, and Santa Fe in 1839. The return trail from Santa Fe in 1840 passed just south of here, roughly paralleling the highway. The route was little used until 1849, when the California gold rush drew immigrants from the east."

The road continues to drop, but more slowly now. At **256 mi.** (48 mi.) you reach **Longhorn Ranch** Cafe and gas station. This is a popular stop for travelers, offering a "museum," cafe, gas, and other accommodations.

US 66 continues to descend, leveling off as you approach **BUFORD**, at **264 mi.** (40 mi.). This small crossroads hamlet offers four cafes, six gas stations, two courts: Yucca and one other.

West of Buford, the road starts climbing again, imperceptibly at first, across the high plains along this stretch. This section is devoted principally to farming, with a few cattle ranches.

274 mi. (30 mi.) **EDGEWOOD.** (Pop. 132; cafes; gas; no tourist facilities.) About a dozen buildings here; the principal business being shipment of pinto beans—a western dish you have probably sampled by the time you've reached this far.

Three miles farther, at **277 mi.** (27 mi.) is **BARTON**, which consists of a gas station, grocery, and a few cabins.

West of Barton, US 66 continues to climb, until you reach the highest elevation east of Albuquerque at **280 mi.** (24 mi.), being up about 7,000 feet. Now the fairly straight road ends, and you start on a winding road for the next 15 miles, as you drop down through **TIJERAS CANYON** to Albuquerque.

281 mi. (23 mi.) Gas station, with cafe and grocery. From here you drop rather swiftly for the next mile. Another gas station at **282 mi.** (22 mi.).

Now US 66 winds downward through the narrowing canyon, with towering mountains on both sides. You will find gas stations at frequent intervals, averaging a little less than two miles apart, the rest of the way into Albuquerque.

At **289 mi.** (15 mi.) you pass the village of **TIJERAS**, nestled in the valley off US 66 to your left a half-mile. After a few more twists and dips, you suddenly come out of Tijeras Canyon, at **295 mi.** (9 mi.). Opening before you is the wide valley of the **RIO GRANDE**, in which the city of Albuquerque is located. You have a wonderful view of the city and surrounding territory at this point, and if it is at night when you approach the city, its myriad lights will resemble an upside-down heaven spread before you. Off to your left is the great **ARMY AIR FIELD**.

Far ahead, to the west, you can see the high western bluffs of the valley, up which you will climb after leaving the city. As you come down out of the canyon and onto the plain you can see three distinct peaks in the distance to your right (northwest). These are the cones of extinct volcanoes.

299 mi. (5 mi.) Pass the entrance (L) to **Albuquerque Army Air Field.** Two miles farther you pass the **New Mexico Fair Grounds** entrance (R). The great fair is held here annually around the end of September or the first of October. It usually lasts a week, and during that time it is virtually impossible to get any accommodations—even tourist cabins in the city.

Now you are entering the city itself. At **304 mi.** (0 mi.) you go beneath a railroad underpass, which ends the speedometer readings for this leg of your journey.

ALBUQUERQUE. (Pop. 35,449; alt. 4,953'; radio stations KGGM—1260 kc., KOB—770 kc.; plenty of garages, hotels, courts, and all types of tourist accommodations.)

US 66 goes through the heart of Albuquerque, but the city is not so large as to present a traffic problem to the traveler. You will find plenty of tourist courts on US 66 both east and west of the city, with a few near the center of town. Courts on the east side include: Pinon Lodge, Lo-La-Mi, Urban Motor Lodge, El Dorado, Tracy's, Rodeo Court, Guest Court, Fair Grounds Court, El Rey, Carrico, De Anza Motor Lodge, Marten's, El Oriente, Coronado, Zia Lodge, Aztec Court. In town is King's Court.

From the center of town out to the Rio Grande River, near the western edge of town, are more courts: Will Rogers, Tower, Texas Ann, Monterey, White Way, Country Club, Moon Motel, El Vado, Pueblo Bonito, and Beach Court.

Across the Rio Grande, at the west edge of the city, are several more courts, including Sundown Trailer Park, Sky, Duke's, Stop-In, Rainbow, Sylvia's, Sandia, Dutch, Navajo, El Compo, Silver King, 66 Court, California, Blue Bell, El Rancho, Mile-Hi, Scott's, Royal, Alamo and many others. The tourist courts in Albuquerque are among the finest along US 66, but because of the housing shortage, many of them are at present apparently occupied constantly, so latecomers may have to hunt for accommodations.

There are several good hotels, including the Franciscan. Hilton, El Fidel, and Alvarado, as well as some smaller ones, including: Combs, Sturges, Elms, Savoy; garages include Galles Motor Co. and Oden Motor Co.

Albuquerque has a population of 65,000 in its Metropolitan area, and is New Mexico's largest city. It is the business center of the state and the home of many regional Government offices. The University of New Mexico is located here, as well as a large Indian school and a U. S. Veterans' Facility.

The town depends greatly on its tourist trade, and there are many fine shops selling authentic Indian craft goods. Large numbers of health seekers come here because of the fine climate. The principal industries of the region include cattle raising, wool growing, mining, timber, and farming.

Within the city limits are many attractions, and the local Chamber of Commerce at 319 N. Fourth St. (three blocks off US 66) will supply folders to guide you. There is the historic "old town," founded in 1705; a municipal bathing beach; zoo; missions; and similar sights. On the streets you will see Indians in their native costumes. Don't fail to visit the fine exhibit of Indian antiques assembled by Fred Harvey, in a building adjoining the Santa Fe station.

In the vicinity of Albuquerque there are many natural and historical attractions. The Sandia Mountain playground area is a short drive away, offering a 70 mile scenic drive, a road to an 11,000 foot crest, picnic grounds, and—in winter—skiing. North of Albuquerque is ancient Santa Fe, the historic state capitol, and Taos, the famous art and literary colony.

South of Albuquerque about 12 miles is Isleta Pueblo, one of the largest in the state. It has an old mission built in 1621, and the Indians today live much as they did in the days when Coronado and other Spanish Conquistadores came here.

Eighteen miles north of the city is the Coronado State Monument, including the excavated ruins of an ancient pueblo. (Small admission charge.)

The various Indian pueblos in the region hold regular dances, which are chiefly religious ceremonies and which draw many tourists. If any of these are in progress during the dates you pass through the region, it is a memorable event worth stopping to see. Incidentally, photography is often prohibited at these dances, but in many cases the local "Governor" of the pueblo will issue a permit for a small fee. It is advisable to take a lunch along.

Following are some of the approximate dates of pueblo dances. Get definite date and directions from Chamber of Commerce in Albuquerque. Feb. 2—Buffalo Dance at San Felipe Pueblo, 6½ mi.; June 13, San Antonio Day at Sandia Pueblo, 13 mi.; July 26, Green Corn Dance at old Santa Ana Pueblo, 23 mi.; Aug. 15, Green Corn Dance at Zia Pueblo, 35 mi.; Sept. 4, Harvest Dance at Isleta Pueblo, 12 mi. Many other dances are held at distances of 50 miles or more from Albuquerque.

This section of your trip over US 66 takes you from Albuquerque, New Mexico, to Holbrook, Arizona. Now truly you are in a fabulous land, for in this part of your trip you will pass ancient pueblos, volcanic lava flows, the Continental Divide, Indian reservations, the Painted Desert, the Petrified Forest, and many Indian trading posts.

At the west edge of Albuquerque is the famous **RIO GRANDE RIVER,** which flows south and then turns southeast to enter the Gulf of New Mexico. "Rio Grande" means "great river," but the river is small compared to eastern torrents. However, for this arid region, it is truly a "great river." Mark your speedometer reading in the margin of this page now, so you can follow the mileage readings given in this Guide Book. **0 mi.** (250 mi.).

West of the Rio Grande, you pass through the western suburbs of Albuquerque. Many tourist courts line the highway along here. Almost at the edge of town, you begin to climb the long, steep grades up out of the Rio Grande valley and onto the plateau. These first grades extend for about three miles, ending at **9 mi.** (241 mi.).

For the next 40 miles, there are only two places where gasoline may be obtained. This section contains several long grades down into valleys and up the opposite side. At the foot of one of these grades, at **19 mi.** (231 mi.) is a gas station.

The road continues to dip and rise until you reach **CORREO** at **33 mi.** (217 mi.). Here there are two establishments, one on each side of a railroad which crosses US 66. Correo (Pop. 10) offers gas, groceries, small cafe, and a few cabins. As in the case with most roadside establishments along here, these places carry a display of curios, jewelry, and Navajo rugs. "Correo" is Spanish for "post-office."

Now the highway enters upon an area of richly colored desert and mesa, upon which herds of sheep and occasionally cattle graze. The vistas stretch interminably into the distance, and the inverted turquoise bowl of the sky becomes a mingling of indescribable colors at sunset.

At **44 mi.** (206 mi.) you will notice **MESITA VILLAGE** off to the right. This cluster of homes is not on US 66 and has no facilities for the traveler.

The road along here is nearly level, climbing imperceptibly and soon entering high mesas, which look like squat, flat-topped mountains rising abruptly from the plains. It was on these mesas that the early Indians built their pueblos for protection, raising their flocks and crops on the plains below. The countryside looks much as it did in the days when Coronado wandered through here seeking the fabled cities of gold. One of the best things the government has done for the Indians has been to sink many water wells.

Incidentally, if you have occasion to photograph any of the Indians by the roadside, do not be surprised if they ask for money for posing. Their "fees" vary, and it has become an established custom to pay them small amounts.

47 mi. (203 mi.) Short, steep hill going up west here, in a cut through a mesa. Shortly west of here is a **garage** (R) by the roadside.

49 mi. (201 mi.) **LAGUNA.** (Pop. 2,451; alt. 5,851 ; gas;

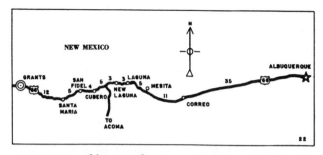

grocery; no cabins or other accommodations.) This is the site of **LAGUNA PUEBLO**, the only major pueblo still visible from Highway 66. Its white structures and church can be seen (L). Laguna is the only pueblo built since the Spanish invasion, its construction having begun around 1800. The houses in the pueblos of this vicinity are made of flat stones, well-plastered with adobe mud. The mission church is a massive stone structure with few windows or other openings. The store at the crossroads is quite a supply center for the Indians. Fiesta around Sept. 19.

Leaving Laguna, the road makes a short, winding climb, and soon comes to the small cluster of homes (L) which comprise **NEW LAGUNA, 52 mi. (198 mi.).** Gas station here.

55 mi. (195 mi.) Paraje Trading Post. This single structure is at the intersection of a road (L) to **ACOMA PUEBLO.** The direction to Acoma is plainly marked, and a visit to this remarkable place is practically a "must." You travel about 14 miles over a graded dirt-and-gravel road to reach it. On the way you pass the **ENCHANTED MESA** about 10 miles from US 66. This mesa (L) was once the site of a village, but its sides fell away during an earthquake, marooning three old women who had been left in the pueblo while the villagers tilled the fields below. The mesa can be climbed by experienced climbers.

When you approach **ACOMA ROCK,** you will have to park your car and climb a sandy, sloping trail to its table-like top. The pueblo covers over 70 acres and is over 350 feet above the surrounding plain. An admission fee of $1 per person is charged, the money going for improvements.

Acoma, known also as the "Sky City," is the oldest pueblo in North America which has been inhabited continuously. In one of the early battles with the Spanish Conquistadores, five soldiers leaped from its height, and all but one lived to tell the tale! Until 200 years ago, the only method of access was by climbing up toe-holds in the rock.

At the top is the pueblo, several structures made of stone and adobe, and still inhabited—although most of the villagers spend the summers in the valley below with their flocks and crops. The old church, the Mission of San Esteban Rey, was started in 1629, and it is the locale of Willa Cather's book, **"Death Comes For the Archbishop."** A ceremonial dance is held here the first week in September of each year. A few years ago, the Walter Wanger studio produced the film "Sundown" here, and in order to make the locale appear African for movie purposes, they brought in several elephants, camels, zebras and other animals, which appeared strange indeed to the natives!

Returning to US 66, you continue westward over countryside that is somewhat rolling. To your right, in the north looms the height of **MOUNT TAYLOR,** snow-capped through most of the year and sacred to the Indians. (Note: The mileage figures in this Guide Book do not include any side trips, such as to Acoma.)

57 mi. (193 mi.) Gas station. Soon you come to **CUBERO,** a small community off US 66 (R). Two roads enter the village from US 66, the western intersection being at **60 mi.** (190 mi.) There is a good cafe and tourist court at Villa de Cubero. Along the road here are gas stations, cafes, stores, a few cabins, but no other accommodations.

West of Cubero, the region appears more desolate. At **61 mi.** (189 mi.) is **Los Cerritos Trading Post.** Gas and grocery here.

64 mi. (186 mi.) **SAN FIDEL.** (Pop. 128; alt. 5,900 ; cafe; gas; small garage; curios; store; no cabins or other accommodations.) San Fidel was originally a busy trading center; today it has declined somewhat.

Along this section of US 66, Indians sit by the roadside selling pottery. For the most part, they do not bargain over prices: each item bears its price marked on the bottom. Most of the pieces are the fragile Acoma ware, white with brown designs. There is an amusing anecdote of how one clever Indian girl retaliated against sharp-bargaining, callous tourists by collecting some cockle-burrs which she sold to a tourist as very rare "porcupine eggs." The tourist bought them!

66 mi. (184 mi.) Chief's Rancho Cafe here, with gas, grocery, curios, and cafe.

69 mi. (181 mi.) **SANTA MARIA** is a small village located off to the left here, with a cluster of adobe homes and a mission church clinging to the rocky side of the mesa. No tourist facilities except a gas station at the highway.

West of here, you enter a lava flow, whose black lava lies in hardened masses on both sides of the road. At **70 mi.** (180 mi.) is a **HISTORICAL MARKER: LAVA FLOW.**

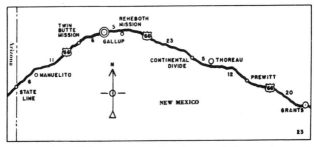

Text reads: "This great lava flow is one of the most recent in the United States, occurring between 1,000 and 2,000 years ago. It extends approximately 40 miles south and west." This lava flow is often called **"The Malpais,"** which means "evil country." In its tortuous area lie deserted pueblos, rumored hidden treasure, caves of perpetual ice, veins of ore, and the hideouts of early bandits. Its exploration is a hardy project, but many of the adventurous attempt it.

81 mi. (169 mi.) **GRANTS.** (Pop. 2,000; alt. 6,641'; hotels: California and Yucca; courts: Lakeside, Encanto, Kimo, Grants and Zia; garage: Conley; stores; cafes; all facilities.) The Indians call Grants **NAHTO-SI-KA'I** (Place of Friendly Smoke), because a treaty was signed here between old Chief Manuelito and Kit Carson. The town began in 1872 as the site of the rancho of Don Blea. It is the key point of an extensive livestock, farming, oil, and lumbering center, and is perhaps most noted for its vegetable crops, of which carrots are most prominent. Carrots from here are shipped to all parts of the U. S. **Mike Croteau's Trading Post** is an interesting place, and Mike himself is full of unusual anecdotes for those who come to know him. Many tourists come to Grants as their "jumping off place" for side trips to the **PERPETUAL ICE CAVES** and **EL MORRO NATIONAL MONUMENT**, which lie to the southwest.

The Ice Caves are about 28 miles from Grants, and contain solid masses of pure, pale blue ice in volcanic caves whose air currents are said to preserve the ice.

El Morro is a towering mass of rock whose base bears famous inscriptions of early Spanish and American explorers, some dating as far back as 1605. Get road directions in Grants.

87 mi. (163 mi.) Vidal's Trading Post. Gas and curios.

90 mi. (160 mi.) Hardenburg Commissary, center of temporary lodging for pickers who come to harvest vegetable crops.

95 mi. (155 mi.) Several trading posts along here include Bowlin's, Pioneer, and Brown's. Myrick Garage here, too.

At 98 mi. (152 mi.) you begin to enter a region of scrub trees, leaving the desert behind. US 66 now climbs slowly.

101 mi. (149 mi.) PREWITT. A small community, including several railroad siding shacks and Prewitt's Trading Post. Just west is the depot of the Petroleum Products Refining Co. Gas station here. No tourist accommodations in Prewitt.

At 102 mi. (148 mi.) you pass the Baca Day School, a few low buildings off US 66 (L).

113 mi. (137 mi.) THOREAU. (Pop. 375.) Thoreau Trading Post and Beautiful Mountain Trading Post here; gas and garage. Thoreau itself lies off US 66 (R).

US 66 continues to climb and dip, continuing upward, and looking backward you get a good view of Mount Taylor. Off to the right are red sandstone cliffs, paralleling US 66 for the next several miles. North of here about 65 miles lies the famous **PUEBLO BONITO**, where the largest known pueblo is being excavated.

118 mi. (132 mi.) **CONTINENTAL DIVIDE.** At this point US 66 crosses the north-south line which geographers have established as the "backbone" of the United States. Water falling east of this line flows into the Atlantic; falling west of the line it flows to the Pacific. The altitude here is 7,263 feet, and it is the highest point on US 66.

At the Divide, which is marked by a large sign, are several establishments: The Top O' The World Hotel & Cafe, Great Divide Trading Co., and the Continental Trading Post and grocery.

Leaving the Divide, US 66 starts to descend in a series of dips. At **121 mi.** (129 mi.) is Fred Wilson's Indian Trading Post. Gas here.

122 mi. (128 mi.) Navajo Trading Co. One establishment: offering gas, cafe, and a few cabins. A few miles beyond, the scrub pines begin to thin out, the dips in the road become less frequent, and a slow descent begins.

133 mi. (117 mi.) Perea Trading Post. Gas here.

136 mi. (114 mi.) The entrance to **FORT WINGATE** is here (L). During World War II, Ft. Wingate served as a large munitions depot and quartermaster center. The Fort was originally established just after the Civil War and was later the location of a Navajo school.

137 mi. (113 mi.) **HISTORICAL MARKER: KIT CARSON**

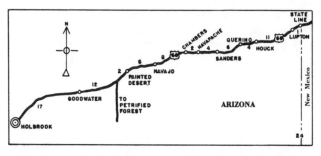

CAVES. Text reads: "3½ miles north. While scouting for Army in the campaign against the Navajos in 1864, Kit Carson camped in this vast sandstone cave. It offered a good vantage point, protection and spring water." The caves are open to visitors, with a small admission charge.

The great, red sandstone bluffs (R) which have paralleled US 66 for many miles, contain a large formation just east of the road to Carson's caves. This formation is known as the **NAVAJO CHURCH**, and is considered sacred by the Indians.

140 mi. (110 mi.) Kirk Brothers Trading Post. Store, no gas, few cabins here.

141 mi. (109 mi.) **REHEBOTH MISSION**, off US 66 (L) a few hundred yards. The mission was established over 40 years ago by the Board of Missions of the Christian Reformed Church, and it maintains an Indian school.

Along this section of US 66, considerable new construction is being made, and you will find short detours along the highway right of way occasionally.

146 mi. (104 mi.) **GALLUP.** (Pop. 7,041; alt. 6,505'; hotels: El Rancho, El Navajo, Delmar, Grand, Liberty; courts:

Casa Linda, Fonda, Log Cabin, All States, La Siesta, La Posada, Jim's, Coronado, Zia, La Hacienda, and others; garages: Frank's and Navajo Chevrolet; many curio stores, cafes, and all other accommodations.)

Gallup is a great Indian trading center, to which they come for supplies and from which Navajo and other Indian wares are shipped. It is also famous for its great **Inter-Tribal Indian Ceremonial** held annually just after the middle of August. The Gallup Ceremonial possibly has a greater attendance and more varied program than any similar event held in any town you will pass through on US 66.

By all means, visit the Ceremonial if you can. It features Indian tribal dances, horse races, demonstrations of Indian blanket weaving, silverworking and sand painting, and other similar events.

Oddly enough, Gallup is also a coal town! The geological formations of the vicinity have exposed veins of coal, and the mines have also caused the development of a brick kiln.

To the north of Gallup lies **SHIPROCK** and the great Indian country. South of the town is a large **ZUNI PUEBLO**, which is open to visitors and holds a festival at the end of the year. The pueblo is 41 miles south of Gallup. In Gallup, an enterprising air service offers flight over the Indian country for tourists interested in seeing this unusual region from the air.

The recent movie, **"Sea of Grass,"** was filmed on location near Gallup in 1946, with Spencer Tracy and Katherine Hepburn as stars.

152 mi. (98 mi.) Twin Butte Nazarene Navajo Mission (L). Gas station nearby.

In the west, the terms "butte" and "mesa" are often used. "Butte" is pronounced like the first syllable in "beautiful," and Webster defines it as "a conspicuous hill or natural turret." "Mesa," pronounced "maysa," is Spanish for "table" and is defined as "a high, broad, and flat table-land, usually with precipitous cliffs descending to the plains."

153 mi. (97 mi.) **New Mexico Port of** Entry (L). Trucks are inspected here. Gas station nearby.

156 mi. (94 mi.) Defiance Trading Post. Gas here. At **158 mi.** (92 mi.) is the Rocky Point Mercantile Co. Gas and grocery.

160 mi. (90 mi.) **HISTORICAL MARKER: CORONADO'S ROUTE.** The text states that Coronado came through here in his search for the "Seven Cities of Cibola." Returning scouts and traders had told Coronado and others of seven cities of gold reported in this region. Coronado never found them, naturally, but in 1946 prehistoric ruins a few miles north of this point were classified as being the cities probably reported by the early travelers.

161 mi. (89 mi.) Dean Kirk's Trading Post. No gas.

163 mi. (87 mi.) **MANUELITO.** (Alt. 6,260'.) This small community of homes, church, and school lies off US 66 (L). The town is named after a Navajo chief, who signed the treaty with Kit Carson in Grants, New Mexico. (No tourist facilities.)

165 mi. (85 mi.) US 66 now runs between narrowing red bluffs on either side, and at this point goes up a slight hill over a shoulder at the foot of **DEVIL'S CLIFF** (R).

At **168 mi.** (82 mi.), the Box Canyon Trading Post (gas)

nestles beneath the cliff. Navajo "hogans" (homes) in the vicinity.

169 mi. (81 mi.) **NEW MEXICO-ARIZONA STATE LINE.** As you pass under an arch, you pass the "State Line Station," which maintains a good cafe, gas station, etc. At once you enter on a wide stretch of Arizona highway, which will extend for the next 12 miles.

170 mi. (80 mi.) **LUPTON.** (Pop. 33; alt. 6,295'; postoffice; gas stations; store; no other facilities.) The **Arizona Port of Entry** is located here, and all trucks must be inspected at this point.

Now the bluffs on both sides of the road begin to separate as you emerge onto a wide area, forested with scrub pines.

173 mi. (77 mi.) Stafford's Cafe, including gas, groceries, and a curio shop, comprises the town of **ALLANTOWN** here. Soon the trees become more sparse, and you begin to enter a stretch of over 125 miles of almost barren country.

181 mi. (69 mi.) **HOUCK.** Two establishments here: the White Mountain Trading Post (which includes a postoffice) and a small curio shop. Gas and groceries here. Navajos are nearly always lounging around the trading post, drinking the soda pop they enjoy. The Navajos are a quiet tribe, whose deft ability in silverwork made them useful in many war plants requiring fine assembly work during the war. They are not allowed to vote, but were subject to the draft in the war.

182 mi. (68 mi.) US 66 passes a colony of Navajo hogans: private dwellings.

183 mi. (67 mi.) Good News Indian Mission. Trading post nearby. No gas here. Gas station at **184 mi.** (66 mi)

185 mi. (65 mi.) **QUERINO.** Another one-structure "town," consisting of the Querino Trading Post. Curios and gas.

186 mi. (64 mi.) Trading post only. No gas here.

188 mi. (62 mi.) A building here houses some excavations of **Indian ruins.** Private enterprise.

189 mi. (61 mi.) Gas station and garage.

191 mi. (59 mi.) **SANDERS.** (Pop. 88; alt. 5,836'.) This town consists of the Tipton Bros. Store and two gas stations.

195 mi. (55 mi.) **NAVAPACHE.** Another small "town" consisting of one tourist court, a gas station, garage and store.

197 mi. (53 mi.) **CHAMBERS.** (Pop. 59.) Consists of one small tourist court, 2 gas stations, Riggs Cafe, and a few buildings.

199 mi. (51 mi.) Indian Village Trading Post. No gas.

201 mi. (49 mi.) Rio Puerco Service station; gas only.

205 mi. (45 mi.) **NAVAJO.** (Pop. 52; alt. 5,634'.) Consists of Marty's Trading Post, with gas and groceries; a small neat cafe in a house back of the trading post, and five tourist cabins.

221 mi. (29 mi.) **PAINTED DESERT.** At this point, you will be able to see the famous Painted Desert, whose soils and rocks are of many colors—blue, chocolate, rose, purple, and many other pastel tints. The colors are best at sunset or at sunrise. This is only one of many such Painted Deserts in this part of Arizona, but this one is the most famous. Indians use the colored sands to make beautiful paintings.

At the above mileage point is a roadside establishment which serves as a bus route stop. It offers gas, cafe, and curios. It has a tower from which the Desert can be seen. Just west of this point is a road (R) which runs two miles north to the PAINTED DESERT INN, built a few years before the war, and offering tourist accommodations and good food. Contains a museum, ranger station, and trading post. Fine view of the Painted Desert from here.

221 mi. (29 mi.) Road left here to **PETRIFIED FOREST**, 5 miles. This is a National Monument, and contains over 90,000 acres of petrified trees. Visitors are now forbidden to carry away any of the wood, because the forests were nearly wiped out by those who first came here and shipped out carloads of the material.

There is a 50c admission charge for autos and for trailers. The area contains camping facilities and picnic areas, and Rainbow Forest Lodge offers a few housekeeping cabins. There is an interesting museum at the park headquarters.

The trees have become petrified over millions of years, and now lie like great jewels—which they are: huge chunks of agate and carnelian, useful for semi-precious stones in jewelry when polished properly. Ancient men lived here, and have left their ruined homes and hieroglyphics.

You can drive off US 66 to the Forest and return, or you can drive through the Forest for 25 miles south and reach US 260, which continues 20 miles west into Holbrook.

Returning to US 66, you continue west. At **225 mi.** (25 mi.) is a gas station and cafe in an old stone structure bearing the sign: "Old Stage Station."

226 mi. (24 mi.) Painted Desert Point. Gas only.

233 mi. (17 mi.) **GOODWATER.** Consists of gas stations, grocery and curio shop.

250 mi. (0 mi.) **HOLBROOK.** (Pop. 1,184; alt. 5,079'; hotels: Arizona, Holbrook, Navajo; courts: Forest, Barth, Navajo, El Moderno, El Sereno, White, El Patio, Central, and El Rancho; garages: Mefford, Heward, and Guttery; good food at Green Lantern Cafe; stores; all facilities.)

Holbrook is now a quiet county seat, but in its early days was a rootin', tootin' cowtown, where the boys could blow off steam accumulated through long, hard days on the range. Today it is quite a tourist center, especially for those who plan a few days' stopover to leisurely visit the Painted Desert, Petrified Forest, and the many Indian villages in the vicinity. Dates of Indian dances and other events can be secured from the local Chamber of Commerce.

·SOME FACTS ABOUT NAVAJO RUGS

Many tourists buy Navajo rugs as souvenirs. There are no "imitation" Navajo rugs—all are genuine, but some are made with cotton warps and are not 100% wool. The Indian weaver receives less than 10c an hour for her work, and it takes about 8 hours to weave a square foot of rug, when you include preparation of the wool. For this reason, rugs are scarce and may be more so.

Navajo rugs wear indefinitely. They may be vacuumed or dry cleaned, but should not be laundered, although small ones may be washed with lukewarm water and Lux.

From Holbrook, Arizona, to Kingman, Arizona, your journey over US Highway 66 climbs to 7,130 feet. You  will pass near pre-historic ruins, wind through the nation's largest stand of pines, and will pass near the tremendous Grand Canyon. In the winter months, you may find sections of the road blocked by heavy snow for short periods, and will encounter frequent ice. Plows clear the roads promptly, but you should use caution in driving, especially at night.

In the center of Holbrook, US 66 makes a right turn and heads almost straight west. **0 mi. (274 mi.)** Mark your speedometer reading in the margin of this page here, so you can follow the mileage readings given in this Guide Book. Adjust figures to allow for variance in your speedometer when necessary, if your calculations reveal a difference.

Heading west from Holbrook, US 66 climbs very slowly for the next 75 miles. At **9 mi. (265 mi.)** you pass some red stone buttes (R), with a service station nestling at their base. On your left is a wide, shallow pond.

15 mi. (259 mi.) JOSEPH CITY. (Pop. 308; alt. 5,080'; courts: Hopi Village and Oasis; gas; garage; store; no cafe or other accommodations.) This town was founded by the Mormons 70 years ago, and some of the old brick homes, of eastern design, may date from that early period. The Mormons struggled valiantly to irrigate the region and establish farms, with some success.

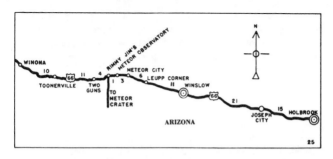

On the level plains west of Joseph City, you enter a region of true Arizona beauty. During many months of the year, great, soft clouds drift across the turquoise sky; the earth is a warm tan; the sunsets are an indescribable riot of vivid colors which change swiftly. Far ahead you can see great peaks, snow-capped much of the year. These are the San Francisco Peaks, ancient volcanoes which are Arizona's highest mountains. You will pass them west of Flagstaff.

Some road maps show two "towns" along here. Both are mere collections of yellow shacks which house railroad workers; neither touch the highway nor even offer a gas station for the motorist: **MANILA**, at **18 mi.** (256 mi.), and **HAVRE**, at **24 mi.** (250 mi.) both on your left.

32 mi. (242 mi.) The "Painted Desert Hideaway," a gas station and cafe.

33 mi. (241 mi.) At this point you cross the **LITTLE COLORADO RIVER**. This river has paralleled US 66 on your left, in the distance, since Holbrook. It provides the chief source of irrigation for the district.

36 mi. (238 mi.) **WINSLOW.** (Pop. 4,577; alt. 4,856′; hospital; hotels: La Posada, Chief, Winslow, Palace, Elk;

courts: Bazell, Drumm's, West End, El Hopi, Union, Camp Keyton, Beacon, Sears Auto Camp; garages: El Gran and Lorenzo Hubbell Motor Co.; cafes; stores; trading posts; all facilities.) Rodeo here early each September.

Winslow is quite a center for tourists, vacationists and health-seekers. Its open air, high altitude, and pleasant climate are combined with its location in the center of many surrounding historic spots: Indian villages, old ruins, and similar points. It is one of the largest towns in Northern Arizona, and is a cattle and railroad center. Lorenzo Hubbell was one of the most famous early Indian traders, and his sons carry on his work here. In the Lorenzo Hubbell Motor Co. showroom is the world's largest Navajo rug: 21 feet by 37 feet. It was made for Mr. Hubbell, and required two years to weave. It weighs 240 lbs.

44 mi. (230 mi.) The "town" of **MOQUI** shown on many maps at this point consists of a railroad siding with a few yellow board shacks.

47 mi. (227 mi.) **LEUPP CORNER.** The Hopi House Service Station is the only building here, with a few Navajo hogans near it. The trader here is an affable, experienced man with a fairly extensive stock.

Another disappointing "town" is **DENNISON,** at **50 mi.** (224 mi.). It consists solely of railroad houses, and offers no tourist facilities, not even gas.

53 mi. (221 mi.) **METEOR CITY.** One building, offering gas, groceries, and curios. For many years, a roadside sign here said "Population 1," but early in 1946 the operator of the "town" married, and the sign now says "Population 2."

US 66 winds around some low hills along this stretch

which is often swept by whipping winds in the spring.

At **56 mi.** (218 mi.) you pass **METEOR CRATER OB-SERVATORY**, a castle-like stone structure on a hill (R). Admission is free, and a stock of curios is for sale. The building houses a model of the **METEOR CRATER**, which lies a few miles south and is visible from the observatory.

The crater is a deep bowl about a mile in diameter and over 700 feet deep, with a low mound heaped around its rim. There is quite a controversy over the crater: for many years it was presumed to be the spot where a great meteor struck at a tangent, entering the earth at an angle about 50,000 years ago. Many attempts have been made to drill down to the meteor—all unsuccessful, but alleged fragments of meteoric mineral have been picked up in the vicinity. In 1946, strong claims were advanced by government scientists that the crater was actually caused by volcanic steam, not by a meteor, and the spot is now marked on all official government maps as **Crater Mound**. The site is owned by an eastern firm.

57 mi. (217 mi.) Rimmy Jim's Service Station. Gas, lunchroom, and a few cabins built to resemble Navajo hogans. Purchase tickets here for Meteor Crater, 4½ miles south. 25c per person.

61 mi. (213 mi.) **TWO GUNS.** One establishment, offering gas, lunchroom, and curios. At the rear of the building is a small zoo exhibiting western animals. In previous years, US 66 ran behind this building, and some old Apache Caves in a canyon there were great showpoints. They can still be visited if you care to walk a few hundred yards back.

62 mi. (212 mi.) Cross **CANYON DIABLO**, an amazing canyon which appears suddenly as a great gash in the

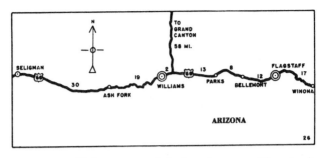

level plain. Unless you watch sharply, you will cross it before you are aware of it. It is over 100 feet deep and several hundred feet wide, although south of here it is deeper. Early wagon-train pioneers found it difficult to cross.

72 mi. (202 mi.) **TOONERVILLE.** A single building providing gasoline, groceries, and lunches. West of here, the plains end, and you soon enter the **COCONINO NATIONAL FOREST.** The first trees are rather scrubby, but they soon give way to tall yellow pines.

74 mi. (200 mi.) US 66 here crosses **PADRE CANYON,** which is quite similar to Canyon Diablo.

Now US 66 winds through the pines, which present a welcome relief from the parched desert. In this region, many ancient pueblos have been found, since the early Indians undoubtedly also enjoyed the timber and shade. Filling station operators between here and Flagstaff can direct you to some of these sites.

82 mi. (192 mi.) **WINONA.** (Alt. 6,005′) **Winona Trading Post** offers cafe, gas, groceries, and several cabins.

US 66 now begins to climb more steeply, although there

are no difficult grades between here and Flagstaff. The pines become taller, and the road winds a bit.

At **86 mi.** (188 mi.) a road runs (L) to **WALNUT CAN-YON STATE PARK,** five miles south. This is one of the major prehistoric ruins easily reached from US 66. In a deep gorge, over 200 cliff dwellings cling to the sides of the steep rock. The village was busiest from 1000 to 1200

A. D., and the people were hunters, farmers, and traders. Open from 8 AM to 5 PM. No admission. Picnic area. Foot trails to many structures.

90 mi. (184 mi.) Gas station. Another at **91 mi.** (183 mi.).

93 mi. (181 mi.) Junction of US 66 and US 89. Camp Townsend Trailer Camp here, with garage and store. You can camp here in the pines.

96 mi. (178 mi.) Camp Elden. Another camping spot, with a garage and cafe.

99 mi. (175 mi.) **FLAGSTAFF.** (Pop. 8,089; alt. 7,000'; hotels: Monte Vista, Weatherford, Bank, Commercial; many courts, including: Arrowhead Lodge, El Pueblo, Flagstaff Motor Village, Rock Plaza, Vandevier Lodge, Nickerson's, Mac's, Motor Inn, Cactus Gardens, Dixon, and Sunset; garages: Cheshire, Babbitt, Waldhan's; curio shops; stores; cafes; all facilities.)

Flagstaff is the locale of the great **All-Indian Pow-Wow** each year for three or more days starting on July 4th and attended by thousands of Indians. Cowboys and Indians can be seen in their picturesque dress on Flagstaff streets the year 'round. Three miles north of here is the **Museum of Northern Arizona,** housing many prehistoric and pioneer relics. Flagstaff is a great trading and lumbering center.

US 66 goes down the main street of Flagstaff, and soon you are on the road among the tall pines again. At **101 mi.** (173 mi.) is Camp Kit Carson. At this point, you strike a stretch of new, wide highway on which you travel for the next 32 miles.

Gas station and cafe at **110 mi.** (164 mi.). Now you are in the eastern end of the **KAIBAB NATIONAL FOREST.**

111 mi. (163 mi.) **BELLEMONT.** (Pop. 141; alt. 7,130'.) This town has the highest altitude of any along US 66. The town includes a store, post office and two gas stations. No other accommodations.

113 mi. (161 mi.) Trading post here; no gas.

119 mi. (155 mi.) **PARKS,** another of those "one establishment towns," offer gas and a few cabins.

120 mi. (154 mi.) Fireside Inn here, with gas and a few cabins.

122 mi. (152 mi.) A tree-shaded camping spot here (L), maintained free by the U. S. Government. Two miles west of here you pass the buildings of the **Challender Ranger Station,** about a half-mile off US 66 to your left.

124 mi. (150 mi.) Wagon Wheel Lodge here offers gas and a few cabins, built of logs.

132 mi. (142 mi.) Junction with paved road north to **GRAND CANYON,** which lies 58 miles north. For information on Grand Canyon, see next page.

GRAND CANYON INFORMATION

Visitors to the Grand Canyon find themselves powerless to adequately describe the magnificent grandeur of this  mighty chasm, which is over 200 miles long, a mile deep and from 4 to 18 miles across.

The Grand Canyon is easily reached over a paved highway from US 66. Naturally, there is no bridge across the canyon itself, although it can be approached from the north over another highway. The two "communities" are known as the North Rim (open from May 30 to September 30) and the South Rim (which you reach from US 66; it is open all year 'round).

There are ample tourist facilities in Grand Canyon Village, on the South Rim, for a short or extended stay. Facilities were curtailed during the war, but have been reopened and increased since the war to accommodate the unprecedented crowds now visiting this awe-inspiring canyon. Facilities include a public auto camp, cabins, hotel, and lodge. Major facilities are under Fred Harvey management. It is advisable to make advance reservations at Bright Angel Lodge and El Tovar Hotel, because of the crowds.

The National Park Service charges an admission fee of $1.00 for each auto entering the Grand Canyon National Park, and the receipts supplement the federal expense of maintaining rangers, roads, and museum here.

Guide trips, mule rides, and other facilities are provided for the visitor. It is possible to get a fine view of the Canyon even though you may be able to spend only an hour or so there.

134 mi. (140 mi.) **WILLIAMS.** (Pop. 2,622; alt. 6,762'; hotels: Fray Marcos, Grand Canyon, and El Pinado; tourist courts: Sal's, West End, Bethel's, Williams Motel, Sun Dial, Mt. Williams, Del Sue, Hull's Motel Inn, Sutton; garages: Williams Motor Co., Gateway, Campbell, and Cheshire; cafes; stores; all accommodations.)

The town gets its name from Bill Williams Mountain, back of the town. Williams was a famous old trapper and scout. Rodeo here at the end of August. An extremely courteous Information Bureau here provides information on Grand Canyon and other nearby scenic points.

From Williams to Ash Fork is 19 miles, but in this distance you drop 1,700 feet down winding grades which are tricky on winter nights when the road is icy. Inquire about road conditions before starting, if driving at night.

135 mi. (139 mi.) Public camp ground here in the pines. At **140 mi.** (134 mi.) is Pine Springs Ranch Lodge, providing gas and a few log cabins.

At **143 mi.** (131 mi.) you start on the downgrade, which winds about 700 feet down in the first 4 miles and then drops another 500 feet in the next 3 miles. There are a few wide curves, but no tricky "switchbacks," though. As you come out on the open slope, you have a magnificent view of the plains ahead. The pines end as you descend, and toward the foot of the grade the road straightens out.

Gas station and store at **150 mi.** (124 mi.); another gas station at **151 mi.** (123 mi.).

153 mi. (121 mi.) **ASH FORK.** (Pop. 600; alt. 5,143'; hotels: Escalante, Arizona, and White House; courts: Hi-Line, Copper State, McCoy's; Theroux garage; cafes; all facilities.) Ash Fork is a trading and supply center for the

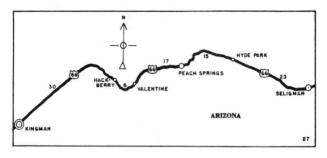

many cattle ranches in the vicinity. Sandstone is also quarried near here.

No gas between Ash Fork and Seligman, about 30 miles distant. The road is fairly straight, across a plain covered with grass and sagebrush.

183 mi. (91 mi.) **SELIGMAN.** (Pop. 500; alt. 5,242′; hotels: Havasu, Navajo, Central, and Seligman; courts: Deluxe and Court Royal; garages: Olson and Seligman; cafes.) Seligman still retains much of its appearance of a cattle town, with its sidewalk awnings and even occasional hitching rails. The town is a railroad section point.

Seligman is the dividing line for another time zone: **Pacific Standard Time** begins here. Westbound travelers should set their watches back one hour at this point (going east advance them an hour), but since Mountain Time is "unofficially" observed even in Kingman, Arizona, it is better to wait until you reach the Arizona-California State line before making the time change.

204 mi. (70 mi.) Deer Lodge cabins and gas. At **206 mi.** (68 mi.) is **HYDE PARK**, offering a cafe, gas, and cabins.

In this region, you enter the **Hualpai Indian Reservation,** home of a tribe whose numbers have been steadily diminishing—in contrast to the Indians in general, whose number is growing. You will see many Hualpai Indians in Peach Springs.

At **217 mi.** (57 mi.) you start down a grade which drops about 250 feet in 2 miles. About halfway down this grade is a sign (R) stating that the lower end of the **Grand Canyon** can be seen in the far distance to the north (R).

Now you drop down through a cleft in the mountains and enter **PEACH SPRINGS**, at **221 mi.** (53 mi.). (Pop. 129; alt, 4,791'; courts: Quamacho, Peach Springs, and Texaco; garage: Milligan; Quamacho Cafe; no hotels; few stores; limited facilities.)

The highway to Peach Springs from Ash Fork has been quite straight, over slightly rolling plains, and the altitude has been dropping steadily. At **234 mi.** (40 mi.) the road begins to wind through **CROZIER CANYON.**

At **236 mi.** (38 mi.) you pass **CROZIER**, a settlement down in the canyon to your left. US 66 previously ran through this canyon community, and the remains of several tourist buildings can be seen. At present, it appears to be a town of railroad homes, distinguishable by their yellow color. There is a swimming pool here.

As you proceed, the canyon becomes more pronounced, and the highway is often cut through solid rock. At **238 mi.** (36 mi.) you pass **VALENTINE** post office. There is a gas station, grocery and a few cabins here.

At **240 mi.** (34 mi.) is the **Valentine Indian School** (R). Long distance telephone station here. The school was built about 45 years ago, and provides education for over 200 Indians from the nearby mountains. (Alt. 3,790'.)

Now, as the road winds around the canyon slopes, the mountains begin to recede, and at **244 mi.** (30 mi.) you reach **HACKBERRY**. (Pop. 94; alt. 3552'.) The town of Hackberry lies down in the valley across the railroad tracks (L). There are several large tanks in the town, which contain the diesel oil used by the locomotives operating on the railroads through here. Along US 66 are 3 gas stations (one offering light repairs) and a lunchroom.

Soon after leaving Hackberry, you leave Crozier Canyon and wind out onto a great plain, on which the road runs amazingly straight into Kingman.

At **265 mi.** (9 mi.) is the entrance (L) to **KINGMAN ARMY AIR BASE**, one of the greatest of our military training bases during World War II. The vast plain, the isolation and the geography of the region offered ideal training conditions. Great bombers and swift fighters operated from here. It was said that the bright moonlight made true night-flying training difficult, though.

267 mi. (7 mi.) Gas station and grocery here. Nearby are homes of many employees of the Kingman Air Base.

274 mi. (0 mi.) **KINGMAN**. (Pop. 2,200; alt. 3,337'; hotels: Beale, Brunswick, Commercial; tourist courts: Akron, Arcadia, Wal-A-Pai, Williams, Kit Carson Motel, Gypsy Garden, Stony Wold, Bungalow, White Rock, Lambert's, Gateway Village, Bell's, Stratton's, Kingman, El Trovatore and Challenger; Modern Trailer Court; garages: Williston & Ireland, Old Trails, and Shanks; cafes; stores; all accommodations.) Guide Book speedometer readings end at the mid-town section of Kingman. Going east, mark your mileage reading in the margin of this page at this point.

All cars going east must stop at the **STATE INSPECTION STATION**, at the eastern edge of Kingman. The purpose of the inspection is to prevent importation of plant diseases and parasites which are unwittingly brought into the state. Arizona officials regret the necessity for such inspection, but the great citrus orchards of the state require careful protection. Officials inspect luggage and cars.

During the war, when the Air Base was active here, all tourist courts were occupied to overflowing, but with the coming of peace the traveler can now find accommodations. Several good cafes in town.

Each September, the citizens of Kingman celebrate their famous "Dig-N-Dogie Days" in a rodeo which combines cowboy contests with miners' events. Since Kingman lies on the margin between the cattle country to the east and the mining country to the west, the event draws a wide audience of local folks as well as many outside visitors. Only "working cowboys" can enter the riding contests, and miners compete to see who can drill a hole fastest. The town takes on quite an old-time, costumed atmosphere during the celebration.

Kingman residents will probably tell you, too, that it was in this town that Clark Gable and Carole Lombard were wed.

Northwest of Kingman, the new Davis Dam is being built across the Colorado River, at a cost of $18 million.

Some west-bound tourists leaves US 66 at Kingman and take US 466, which runs northwest from Kingman to Boulder Dam (the road runs across the top of the wall of the dam), to Las Vegas, Nevada, and then turns southwest and rejoins US 66 at Barstow, California, about 135 miles east of Los Angeles.

CHAPTER X
KINGMAN, ARIZONA, TO LOS ANGELES, CALIF.

On this, the last leg of your route over US Highway 66, you climb one of your steepest grades, wind through rocky

mining country, cross the Colorado River and the scorched Mojave Desert, pass close to volcanoes, and finally drive through cool orange groves and vineyards into Los Angeles.

As you leave **KINGMAN**, Arizona, you come to a fork at the west side of town where US 466 turns north and US 66 turns southwest. **0 mi.** (369 mi.) Mark your speedometer reading in the margin of this page, so you can follow the mileage figures in this chapter.

For the first 5 miles west of Kingman, US 66 climbs slightly and passes through **SITGREAVE PASS**, whose rocky, palisaded walls narrow and then widen as you emerge upon a wide plain. This country is the home of the Mojave and Hualpai Indians, who fell upon early immigrant trains through the pass, one notable massacre occurring about 1862.

At **6 mi.** (363 mi.), you leave the pass. On your left, across the railroad tracks, is a ruined mine structure of rusty corrugated iron. Gas station at **8 mi.** (361 mi.).

Now the road runs straight ahead for 13 miles, down a slight slope for most of the distance. The plain is dotted with mesquite, greasewood, and yucca. Watch out for cattle on the open range here.

At **18 mi.** (351 mi.) you pass Fig Springs Camp, abandoned as this Guide Book goes to press. Here you start the climb up the **Black Mountains** ahead.

Now you start up the **Gold Hill Grade,** possibly the steepest grade you will encounter on US 66. The east side of this grade rises 1400 feet in 9 miles, starting with a long, gentle slope and becoming more difficult as you near the summit. In the last half mile there are two or three quick hairpin turns. The west side of this grade is the steepest, but will present no problem to the westbound driver, who should, however, keep his car in second gear going down.

On your way up the eastern side, you pass two camps: Cool Springs Camp at **23 mi.** (346 mi.), offering gas and a few cabins, and Ed's Camp at **24 mi.** (345 mi.), offering gas.

At the **Gold Hill Summit, 27 mi.** (342 mi.), is a gas station and ice cream parlor. (Alt. 3515′.) Just west is a lookout, with a space where you can park your car to observe the view.

Now you drop down the twisting west side of the Gold Hill Grade, around several sharp turns. The road descends over 700 feet in the 2 miles from the summit into the town of **GOLDROAD,** at **29 mi.** (340 mi.) (Pop. 718; garage; no cabins, cafe or other facilities here.) Goldroad is a small mining community, with gold mines in operation.

For eastbound cars which cannot make the Gold Hill grade, a filling station in Goldroad offers a tow truck which will haul your car to the summit. At last inquiry their charge was $3.50, but may be higher. Cars with trailers may need the service.

Leaving Goldroad, US 66 continues to descend rather swiftly, twisting around the mountains. To the north (R)

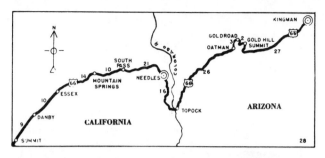

there is a grand view of the mountains, which are desolate, majestic, sun-baked desert peaks.

You pass the Consolidated Gold Mining Company's mine and soon afterwards enter **OATMAN** at **32 mi.** (337 mi.) (Pop. 737; alt. 2,500'; Everett Hotel; two small tourist courts; Bill's garage; limited facilities.) Oatman is a mining boom town whose day has passed, although a few mines still operate. US 66 passes through the town's one main street. Along one side are boarded-up stores, plank sidewalks, old sidewalk awnings. There are many old shacks in the town, dating from its boom at the turn of the century. One store sign says, "We carry general merchandise—nearly all guaranteed." The old Arizona Hotel, still operating, is a truly pioneer structure. Celebration here every Labor Day.

Leaving Oatman, US 66 descends a long, gentle slope into the valley of the Colorado River. The highway passes close to towering peaks. At **35 mi.** (334 mi.) is a trailer camping spot (R), where the ground is level.

37 mi. (332 mi.) **Water faucet** at the roadside here (R) for cars that need water on the climb driving east.

39 mi. (330 mi.) Another spot to stop overnight with a

111

trailer, on the site of a burned-out gas station (L).

45 mi. (324 mi.) Patches of ocotillo cactus along the road here, with tall, slender stalks rising in clusters.

US 66 now winds and dips through a section strewn with boulders of volcanic origin. Their glossy, dark surface  results from action of the fierce sun over many centuries and is called "desert varnish."

Soon you are near the Colorado River and turn south along its eastern bank. Here, among the willows are many quiet spots for campers and fishermen. At **58 mi.** (311 mi.) you reach **TOPOCK.** (Pop. 52; alt. 500′; gas; grocery; few cabins; garage for light repairs; limited facilities.) Now you are down to the lowest elevation you have reached so far on US 66. Topock is an oil distributing center.

At the western edge of Topock, you cross a steel bridge over the **COLORADO RIVER.** Boulder Dam is on this river, far to the north. At the middle of the bridge, you cross the **ARIZONA-CALIFORNIA STATE LINE.**

On the California side of the river, US 66 climbs a few short, steep grades onto a plateau, over which the highway runs into Needles. Between the river and Needles is the site of the great **DESERT TRAINING CENTER,** where U. S. troops trained for the North African campaign in World War II. At one time, 90,000 men were encamped here, practicing desert warfare. Units included infantry, artillery, and tank and other armored outfits. General Patton was one of the first commanders here. The units ranged across the wide desert for many miles, and the maneuver areas are still posted with signs warning against mines and unexploded ammunition. Hunters and prospectors still find abandoned jeeps and other equipment, and recently found the body of an officer who had died of thirst when he became lost. Tracks of the armored vehicles can still be seen on the hills along the road.

59 mi. (310 mi.) Gas station here. Another gas station and coffee shop at **69 mi.** (300 mi.).

74 mi. (295 mi.) **NEEDLES.** (Pop. 3,624; alt. 483´; hotels: California, Gateway, El Garces, Monarch; courts: Monarch, West End, Gray's, Swain's, The Palms, Havasu Court & Trailer Camp, Motor Inn Motel; garages: Old Trails, California, Howard, and Johnson; cafes; stores; all facilities.) Needles is named for a group of sharply pointed peaks in the Black Mountains of Arizona. The peaks are southeast of Needles and are visible when driving east, just before you cross the Colorado River. The town was jammed during the war training period, but is now returning to its leisurely way of life again. Local folk lounge in the plaza, with its cool trees: palm, cottonwood, pepper; and Mojave Indians and Mexicans are often seen. The town is a railroad and trading center. Many mines are located in nearby mountains.

Leaving Needles, you drive along the west bank of the Colorado a short way and then turn west to climb a long slow grade up through the mountains. At **95 mi.** (274 mi.) you reach **SOUTH PASS**, high in the Sacramento Mts. (Alt. 2,650´.) Gas station is the only establishment here.

In the hot months, it is advisable to make the drive from Needles to Barstow, over the Mojave Desert, either in the evening, night, or early morning hours. In any case, it is advisable to carry extra water for the car.

113

Now US 66 descends a straight, 5-mile stretch and climbs for an equal distance to reach **MOUNTAIN SPRINGS** at **105 mi.** (264 mi.). (Alt. 2,700'.) Here you will find one establishment offering gas, lunchroom, and a few cabins, also a small garage. Water is hauled here, so there is a charge for water unless you purchase gasoline. In the valley between South Pass and here, you passed under a power line from Boulder Dam. By the roadside are the neat cottages of the maintenance workers.

US 66 now descends a long, easy slope into the **MOJAVE DESERT**. Once this region lay beneath a great sea, but violent earth movements and volcanic action created many sharp peaks. Through the hundreds of centuries, these peaks eroded and formed the wide valley of this great desert. It is a region of memorable desolation and shimmering heat, yet after its occasional rains the floor of the desert is dotted with flowers. Occasionally you pass "dry lakes" where water collects during rain and later evaporates, leaving mineral salt deposits behind.

119 mi. (250 mi.) **ESSEX.** (Pop. 55; alt. 1,720'; gas; lunchroom; small grocery; post office.) Like so many of the small places along US 66 through the Mojave Desert, Essex chiefly serves the needs of the tourists.

For the next 100 miles, there will be scarcely any change in the scenery. Mountain ranges parallel the highway—each cluster of mountains having its own name. Far ahead lie the San Gabriel Mountains, beyond which lies the orange grove country which so many people consider the true California.

129 mi. (240 mi.) **DANBY.** (Alt. 1,235'.) A gas station, store, and a garage providing light repairs.

138 mi. (231 mi.) **SUMMIT.** (Alt. 1,250'.) A handful of

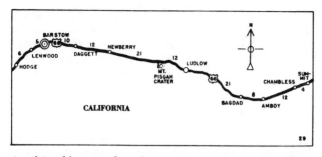

tourist cabins, a cafe and gas station comprise this desert oasis.

142 mi. (227 mi.) **CHAMBLESS.** (Alt. 800'.) A wide-porched gas station, with a cafe and several tourist cabins. One of the few shady spots in the entire desert route. Except for Ludlow, California, there are no "towns" which merit the definition between Needles and Daggett, California, a stretch of 150 miles. Across the road from Chambless is an artillery range used for training during the war.

154 mi. (215 mi.) **AMBOY.** (Pop. 264; alt. 615'.) This desert community consists of two cafes, a garage and a cafe—nothing else. A popular tourist stop. Just west of Amboy is **AMBOY CRATER,** an extinct volcano, whose lava flow touches US 66 about 2 miles west of town. There is a footpath to the top of the crater, providing an opportunity to actually visit a volcano.

US 66 continues across the desert, occasionally passing the remains of burned-out gas stations. Occasionally a mine can be seen in the far distance, at the foothills of a brown mountain range. Skeletons of abandoned cars are frequent along the roadside.

162 mi. (207 mi.) **BAGDAD.** (Pop. 25; alt. 788'.) Except

115

for a few railroad shacks, this community consists solely of a service station, cafe, garage, and a few tourist cabins, all operated by one management. At one time, Bagdad was a roaring mining center. Between 1875 and 1910 the mountains of the Mojave were extensively exploited for their deposits of copper, silver, borax, gold, and other minerals. Great wagon trains hauled freight and ore, and boom towns arose and died quickly.

183 mi. (186 mi.) **LUDLOW.** (Pop. 170; alt: 1,782'.) Although quite small, Ludlow appears to be a real town in comparison to the one-establishment places passed on the way here from Needles. It offers a garage, motels, cafe, ind gas station. Ludlow is still a busy little center, providing supplies for nearby mines. At one time, narrow-gauge railroads ran north from here to Death Valley mines.

US 66 continues westward through the desert. To many easterners, the desert is a terrifying thing, but to many who frequent the region the desert is a thing of majestic beauty. There are many desert lovers, who find its scenery, minerals, history and pioneer lore a fascinating interest. If the desert becomes your "hobby" as well, you should become acquainted with an excellent publication: DESERT MAGAZINE, which describes routes to points of interest in California, Arizona, and New Mexico.

195 mi. (174 mi.). Here you pass close to **MOUNT PISGAH VOLCANIC CRATER,** whose lava flow comes to the very edge of US 66 (L). If you did not visit Amboy Crater, it is worth your while to stop for a few minutes to walk over and examine this lava flow. It is possible but difficult to climb the crater itself.

197 mi. (172 mi.). At this point you pass under a power transmission line. Just east of the transmission line and on the south (L) side of the highway, you will find the ground littered with semi-precious stones: agate and jasper predominating. Of little value in the raw state, these stones make excellent rings, brooches and pins when properly ground and polished.

205 mi. (164 mi.) Gas station, with cafe, few cabins, and garage for light repairs. Similar, but lacking a garage, is another establishment at **206 mi.** (163 mi.).

207 mi. (162 mi.) At this point you pass **TROY DRY LAKE** on the north side of the highway (R), with an airplane beacon (L). After rains, this is actually a shallow lake.

Gas station with garage and tow car at **211 mi.** (158 mi.). Two more gas stations, one with a garage, at **213 mi.** (156 mi.). The desert in this vicinity is dotted with frequent small ranches.

216 mi. (153 mi.) **NEWBERRY.** (Pop. 52; alt. 1,830′.) Nestling at the foot of the cliffs of Newberry Mountain is the single establishment which comprises this town: a gas station with a cafe, grocery, several tourist cabins, and a post office. Behind the cafe is a small swimming pool, closed during the war but now to be reopened. The spot is cool and shady.

Just west of Newberry, the railroad is demolishing an entire mountain, crushing the rock to provide ballast for the tracks.

At **224 mi.** (145 mi.) you pass the **Daggett Air Field** (R), home of the 444th Army Air Force Bombardment Unit during World War II.

228 mi. (141 mi.) **DAGGETT.** (Pop. 245; alt. 2,006′.) As

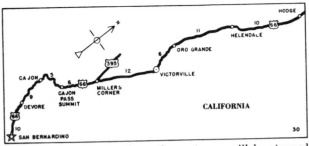

you approach Daggett from the east, you will be stopped at the **CALIFORNIA INSPECTION STATION**, located at this point to check cars coming from the east. Here all westbound cars are stopped and careful inspection made to prevent unwitting importation of fruit and plant diseases and parasites.

The inspection is quite thorough: you will probably be asked to open all suitcases, untie all parcels, and unlock rear trunk compartments for inspection. The state has expressed regret at being compelled to make this inspection, but the great citrus and vegetable industries of the state make it imperative that a check be made. Even a few disease-bearing fruits or plants can multiply quickly. Keep the admission certificate they give you.

Daggett itself is a tree-shaded little old town that was formerly the location of smelters which handled the ore brought down from nearby mountains. Some of the old store buildings remain, but the town is now quiet. There are two trailer camps but no cabins. Cafes, garage, and gas stations.

232 mi. (137 mi.). Here US 66 passes the mile-long area of the **Marine Corps Supply Depot**. The stockpiles which once towered high when the war in the Pacific was at its crescendo are now dwindling.

118

You are now leaving the vast desolation of the Mojave and are entering a region in which many small towns lie close together. The nearby Mojave River provides enough water to enable shade trees to grow in these towns, although there is still bare desert between. The region is full of dude ranches, small farms, and "desert hideaways."

At **235 mi.** (134 mi.) you pass the Greystone Auto and Trailer Camp (L).

238 mi. (131 mi.) **BARSTOW.** (Pop. 2,500; alt. 2,106′; hotels: Beacon Tavern, Melrose, Casa del Desierto, Drumm, Jordan, and Ray; many tourist courts, including: Richfield Cottages, California Inn Camp, 91 Motel, Hollon Motel, Barstow, Henning, Kelly, Clover Leaf, La Casa, Barstow Oasis, Hav-A-Nap, Blythe, Cottonwood, Casa Loma, Kail; garages: Barstow, Pontiac, Dean & Lawson, McMullin and Boucher; cafes; stores; hospitals; all facilities.)

From 1870 to 1900 and later, Barstow was a busy supply point for prospecting expeditions and for Death Valley mine operators. Great wagon trains rolled out daily to nearby mining towns. It was also a "wide-open" center to which miners and others came for relaxation. Today, it is a busy little town with a modern atmosphere, and while it still supplies miners and ranchers, it is a great tourist center and also a railroad center where giant diesel engines are repaired.

At the western edge of Barstow is a hill which appears to mark the edge of town. Unseen beyond this hill, however, are more tourist courts, garages, and cafes.

Heading west from Barstow, you continue on a plateau that rises slowly toward the distant San Gabriel Mts. In the next 40 miles, you will pass through five towns. The first of these, at **243 mi.** (126 mi.) is **LENWOOD.** (Pop. 181;

alt. 2,240'; no hotel; courts: West Barstow, Lenwood, and Radio; Lenwood Service Garage; two cafes; mineral shop.)

Through this section are many chicken and turkey ranches, small farms, and occasional orchards in the valley bottom along the **Mojave River** (R).

249 mi. (120 mi.) **HODGE.** (Pop. 225; alt. 2,160'; only business establishment is a gas station with cafe and a few cabins.) Railroad maintenance crews live in this quiet little desert center.

255 mi. (114 mi.) Old Trails Service station here, also providing groceries and minor auto repairs. No cabins.

Here the Mojave River can be seen quite near US 66. This odd river runs underground for much of its length, appearing suddenly along here. In California, along the coast, the palms and other trees are green the year around, but the cottonwoods along the Mojave River "observe the seasons" and their leaves turn color in autumn.

259 mi. (110 mi.) **HELENDALE.** (Pop. 170; alt. 2,450'.) In one building here are the post office, store, and gas station. Nearby is a state highway maintenance station. Considerable alfalfa is grown in the vicinity, and there is some small-scale mining.

White-Orange Motel is at **262 mi.** (107 mi.) with a gas station just west, offering minor repairs. At **264 mi.** (105 mi.) is a cafe and garage.

Off to the right, high bluffs can be seen in the distance, on the far bank of the Mojave River. Pre-historic Indians lived in the region west of here, and the Mojave Desert appears today much as it did in those long-gone times.

120

At **266 mi.** (103 mi.) is a gas station with cafe and a few cabins. A similar establishment one mile west, at **267 mi.** (102 mi.). The countryside is now often greener.

270 mi. (99 mi.) **ORO GRANDE.** (Pop. 305; alt. 2,631'.) This town, whose name means "great gold," had a population seven times its present size when the nearby gold mines were busy, about 70 years ago. Today its only major industry is a large cement plant which you pass (L). Across from the cement plant are the "company homes" of drab yellow. The town contains about 10 stores, but offers no tourist facilities except one trailer camp with a few cabins.

At **272 mi.** (97 mi.) you cross the Mojave River and climb a short grade to enter the environs of Victorville. At **273 mi.** (96 mi.) is a road (R) to the **Victorville Army Air Field.** Just ahead, to your left, is the switching station and tall towers of the Victorville Station of the Los Angeles Municipal Power & Light Co., bringing power from Boulder Dam. Two miles farther, you pass the big plant (L) of the Southwestern Portland Cement Co., the chief industry of Victorville.

276 mi. (93 mi.) **VICTORVILLE.** (Pop. 3,000; alt. 2,714'; several tourist courts, small hotels, garages, cafes and all tourist facilities.) Mormon pioneers came through here a decade after the Civil War, and 10 years later the town was a hustling mining center. Today it is a resort and farming center. Once there were many orchards here, but now it is devoted to turkey ranches and potato farms. Many western movies have been filmed here "on location," ranging from early Bill Hart films to recent "talkies." Stars such as Pat O'Brien, Tom Mix, and many others have been in films made here. The town holds a horse and stock show early each June. During the war, it was a recreation center for soldiers from the big airfield nearby.

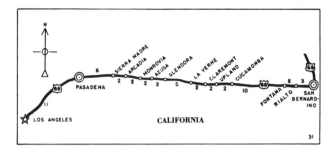

Heading west from Victorville, you enter **BALDY MESA**, named for the tall peak visible to the southwest (L). Here are many Joshua trees, twisted, shaggy plants. The region is full of cabins built by city folk who find a desert weekend a pleasant diversion.

From Victorville west, you climb slowly for 18 miles to the summit of **CAJON PASS**. Along the way are several gas stations, one of the best establishments being at **288 mi.** (81 mi.), at "Millers' Corners." At **290 mi.** (79 mi.) is a junction with US 395, and at **293 mi.** (76 mi.) you enter the **SAN BERNARDINO NATIONAL FOREST.** During the dry summer months, no smoking is allowed—even in cars—for the next 15 miles, because of fire hazards.

At **294 mi.** (75 mi.) you reach **CAJON SUMMIT.** Gas station here. US 66 then begins to descend through deep cuts in the rock, and winds around to the right in a great descending sweep. This is Cajon Pass, famous gateway to Southern California, used for over 100 years. As you descend (sometimes it is necessary to use second gear for safety), you get wonderful, changing vistas of green valleys and mountain ranges in various shades of blue.

At **298 mi.** (71 mi.) is the town of **CAJON**, providing gas and lunchroom. Other gas stations are found frequently along the route of descent. At **299 mi.** (70 mi.) is a junction with State Road 2, which runs left to **Lake Arrowhead,** one of the leading mountain resorts of the region.

US 66 continues downgrade, past the gas station and store at **DEVORE,** at **307 mi.** (62 mi.), and reaches a fork at **315 mi.** (54 mi.), where City 66 runs (L) to **San Bernardino,** and Alternate 66 goes (R) to Los Angeles.

Since this Guide Book is primarily written for the traveler to Los Angeles, it is assumed that you will take the right

(alternate) fork, through the edge of San Bernardino. At the center of a small business district US 66 turns right and heads almost straight west toward Los Angeles, about 53 miles distant.

From this point on, the traveler is practically "in" Los Angeles. Tourist camps of the best type, fine cafes, and other roadside facilities are found all along the way, so no further detailed description is necessary.

Enroute you will pass through 12 small communities before reaching Pasadena. Many of these are so close together as to be practically indistinguishable from each other.

At **318 mi.** (51 mi.) you reach **RIALTO,** a town of about 2,000; at **320 mi.** (49 mi.) you pass through one edge of **FONTANA,** where Henry Kaiser built the first steel blast furnace west of the Rockies, during World War II.

Now you pass through vineyard country and orange groves, through **CUCAMONGA,** at **329 mi.** (40 mi.), **UPLAND,** at **332 mi.** (37 mi.), and **CLAREMONT,** at **334 mi.** (35 mi.).

123

All of these suburbs of Los Angeles are served by electric trains running from the metropolis.

More towns you pass through include **LA VERNE**, at **336 mi.** (33 mi.); **GLENDORA, 241 mi.** (28 mi.); **AZUSA, 343 mi.** (26 mi.); **DUARTE, 347 mi.** (22 mi.); **MONROVIA, 350 mi.** (19 mi.), and **ARCADIA, 352 mi.** (17 mi.). Just west of Arcadia, you pass the **PONY EXPRESS MUSEUM** (L), containing a historic collection of stagecoaches and old western relics. Famous **SANTA ANITA RACETRACK** is just beyond.

Now you pass through **SIERRA MADRE**, at **353 mi.** (16 mi.) and soon enter **PASADENA**, at **359 mi.** (10 mi.). Pasadena is famous for its Rose Bowl, Tournament of Roses, and the Pasadena Playhouse.

From Pasadena, you drive over city streets into **LOS ANGELES**, where you reach the City Hall at **369 mi.** (0 mi.). As was stated in the introduction to this Guide Book, no detailed directions to large cities are given, hence the GUIDE BOOK ends its directions at this point. If you wish to make a **complete** trip over all of US 66, you will have to drive west through **BEVERLY HILLS** to the shore of the Pacific Ocean at **SANTA MONICA**, about 17 miles from the Los Angeles City Hall. There US 66 ends.

In closing, the author hopes you had a pleasant trip. If you have any suggestions on improving this Guide Book, address them to the publisher, so they can be included in future editions.

THE END

THE LOG OF OUR TRIP OVER US 66

(Keep a record of your trip on the lines below:)

Place of Departure..

Date of Departure..

Destination ....

Date of Arrival...

Speedometer R ading at Departure...............................

Speedometer Reading Upon Arrival..............................

Miles Traveled....................Days En Route.....................

Names of Members of Party..

....

Auto Operation:............gallons gasoline, total cost............

............quarts oil, total cost.................Repairs cost............

Total car expense..

Make, model, and year of car driven.............................

Amount spent for meals...................For lodgings..................

Remarks: ....

....

....

WHERE WE HAD GOOD FOOD

WHERE WE HAD GOOD LODGINGS

RECORD OF GAS AND OIL EXPENSES

MISCELLANEOUS	GAS	OIL	COST	GAS	OIL	COST
TOTALS						